Current Chinese Economic Report Series

More information about this series at http://www.springer.com/series/11028

Center for Macroeconomic Research
of Xiamen University

China's Macroeconomic Outlook[1]

Quarterly Forecast and Analysis Report, September 2014

[1] Key Research Institutes of Humanities and Social Sciences of the Ministry of Education of China; National Social Science Foundation of China; Youth Project of the National Social Science Foundation of China.

Springer

Center for Macroeconomic Research of Xiamen University
Xiamen University
Xiamen, Fujian, China

ISSN 2194-7937 ISSN 2194-7945 (electronic)
Current Chinese Economic Report Series
ISBN 978-3-662-45404-6 ISBN 978-3-662-45405-3 (eBook)
DOI 10.1007/978-3-662-45405-3

Library of Congress Control Number: 2014956084

Springer Heidelberg New York Dordrecht London

Printed on acid-free paper

Springer is part of Springer Science+Business Media (www.springer.com)

Preface

This report is a regular serial result of the "China Quarterly Macroeconomic Model (CQMM)," a project of the Center for Macroeconomic Research (CMR) at Xiamen University. The CMR is one of the Key Research Institutes of Humanities and Social Sciences of the Ministry of Education of China. The research is funded by the National Social Science Foundation of China (13&ZD029), the Youth Project of the National Social Science Foundation of China (13CJL017), and the Key Research Institutes of Humanities and Social Sciences of the Ministry of Education of China (14JJD790007, 13JJD790026, 13JJD790025, 12JJD790001).

Since the launch of CQMM 8 years ago, 16 forecast reports with policy simulations and 9 essay collection books on China's macroeconomic analysis have been published. This is the 17th forecast report, which is a summary of the forecast results to be released at the "2014 International Symposium on China's Macroeconomy and CQMM (Autumn) Press Conference on Macroeconomic Projections for 2014–2015." The Symposium will be jointly organized by the Center for Macroeconomic Research, Xiamen University, Springer Press and the Economic Information Daily, Xinhua News Agency in Heidelberg, Germany, on September 11–12, 2014.

Xiamen, China

Center for Macroeconomic Research
of Xiamen University

Contents

Contributors

Principal Investigator

Li Wenpu Center for Macroeconomic Research of Xiamen University, Xiamen University, Xiamen, Fujian, China

Team Members

Lu Shengrong, Gong Min, Li Jing, Wang Yanwu, Chen Guifu, Liu Yu, Xie Pan, Cai Qunqi, Huang Yanping, Wu Huakun, Li Hao, Liang Zhenjie, Miao Xinyue, Xiong Ying, Zheng Jianqing, Chen Tingting, Lao Kaijun, You Yunxing, Zhai Ke.

Chapter 1
Introduction

In the first half year of 2014, China's economic growth kept slowing down compared with the same period of the last year. The GDP growth rate was 7.4 %, the lowest record for the past 4 years. Though the growth of infrastructure construction investment achieved the target of rapid increase, it only partially offset the decline in fixed assets investment growth. However, the decreasing investment growth of manufacturing industries and real estate sector[1] resulted in the slowdown of the real economy. Owing to excess production capacity of manufacturing industries and the huge inventory in real estate sector, it is hard for the governments to realize their ambitious target merely using the micro-stimulus and targeted easing policies.[2] In addition, local governments are heavily in debt and this year will be their repayment peak.

In the second half year of 2014, in spite of all kinds of stimulus polices aiming at facilitating the private capital investment, it is quite uncertain whether these stimulus polices will take effects or not. We predict that the declining trend of investment growth and economy growth will continue, and the urban fixed assets investment[3] will grow by 17.12 % in 2014, a dramatic drop of 2.57 percentage points over previous year, which can mainly be attributed to the shrink of real estate industry. As a result, the GDP growth rate is expected to fall by 7.49 %. In 2014, inflation is likely to remain low, and the CPI is predicted to increase to 2.51 %.

In 2015, the growth rate of GDP is predicted to continue going down to 7.37 %. Since the growth of broad money supply (M2) of 2014 will exceed 14 %, which is much higher than the target set in the beginning of the year, and higher than that of 2013, the CPI will further increase to 2.80 % in 2015 under the condition that economy growth continues going down. In addition, the producer price index (PPI)

[1] The main factors of the economic performance.

[2] This is a more targeted, more restrained kind of stimulus. It is small compared with the massive stimulus of 2008–2009, which cost 4 trillion CNY, but was followed by much more in spending projects initiated by local governments.

[3] Calculated at current price.

CMR of Xiamen University, *China's Macroeconomic Outlook*,
Current Chinese Economic Report Series, DOI 10.1007/978-3-662-45405-3_1

will remain negative in the next 2 years. Though the producer price level kept going down, it had decreased more and more slowly for consecutive 4 months since March 2014, and the trend will continue. PPI is predicted to be −1.53 % and −0.98 % in 2014 and 2015, respectively.

The recovery of the US economy and the mild uncertainty of the Euro-zone economy will promote the growth of China's imports and exports. In 2014, the gross exports[4] will increase by 5.15 %, a drop of 2.97 percentage points over last year. The gross imports will decrease by 5.52 %, a drop of 1.71 percentage points over last year.

Macroeconomic performance in the past 3 years implies the following findings: (1) Within each year, there existed a cyclical economic growth pattern: "decline—micro-stimulus—rebound—decline", and the length of the each cycle is becoming short year after year. (2) The micro-stimulus and targeted easing policies could only relieve the downward pressure of growth of infrastructure investment with very limited effect. In the past 3 years, these stimulus policies mainly concentrated on infrastructure investment and government-subsidized housing: to launch infrastructure investment projects like railway, highway, municipality, energy, environmental protection and water conservancy, where private capital participation was encouraged; to boost the construction of government-subsidized housing, the reconstruction of the rundown urban areas. (3) For each year, the starting time of the implementing the stimulus policies had to be shifted to an earlier month, from the third quarter in 2012 to the middle of 2013, and then to the second quarter of 2014. (4) The marginal effect of such stimulus policies on economic growth is diminishing. With the micro-stimulus policies, the growth rate increased by 0.5 percentage point in 2012, by 0.3 percentage point in 2013, and by 0.1 percentage point in 2014.[5]

In conclusion, in the past 3 years, the central government kept applying the micro-stimulus and targeted easing policies to relieve the downward pressure of China's economy on a growth target above 7.5 %. The results of such policies are: Within each year, there existed a cyclical economic growth pattern: "decline—micro-stimulus—rebound—decline", and the length of the each cycle is becoming short year after year. The marginal effect of such stimulus policies on economy growth is diminishing.

Macroeconomic performance in the past 3 years has showed that, if there were no such micro-stimulus policies, the economic growth rate would have been even lower, but it is not wise to apply micro-stimulus policies frequently in the future, because the short term demand stimulation will only help to smooth the fluctuation in the short run rather than to promote the economic growth in the long run, especially when the natural growth rate[6] of economy is significant lower than the growth target. Frequently applying the micro-stimulus policies to maintain an economic

---

[4] Calculated at current USD.

[5] The growth rate increased from the 7.4 % in the third quarter to the 7.9 % in the fourth quarter in 2012, from 7.5 % in the second quarter to 7.8 % in the third quarter in 2013, from 7.4 % in the first quarter to 7.5 % in the second quarter in 2014.

[6] Steady state growth rate.

growth target higher than the natural growth rate will definitely lead to a high cost of macroeconomic controls and operations, and finally the loss will outweigh the gain.

Based on the features of economic circle, economic development, and the economy of "the new normal", China should reduce its economic growth target, which will be conducive to appropriately reducing the government intervention of market, and help to cut the cost of macroeconomic controls and operations. Thus, we need to investigate the effects of reducing the economic growth target by giving up micro-stimulus policies on other major macroeconomic indicators. Therefore, the goal of our policy simulation is the effects of reducing the economic growth target on the major macroeconomic indicators.

In the simulation, the economic growth rate was imaginatively reduced from 7.7 % down to 7.2 % in 2012 and 2013. Accordingly, to achieve such new growth target, the money supply could have been reduced, too.[7] Such a change of growth target would have negative effect as well as positive effects on investment and consumption. On one hand, the investment would have decreased, employment level would have declined and the resident income growth rate would have dropped owing to less money supply. On the other hand, the reduction of money supply growth rate would have also made price level go down, increased resident real income level and thus promoted residential consumption.

In addition, reducing economic growth target in these 2 years would have produced positive effect on the market economy. Lower growth target could have mitigated the investment incentives of local governments, reduced the scale of the local government financing, given place to the private investment, improved efficiency of private investment, and therefore increased private investment, improved the level of employment, and boosted the residential income. By comparing the positive with the negative effect, the total effect on major macroeconomic indicators would be positive.

Now turning to details, the simulation indicates that if the central government had reduced the economic growth target to 7.2 % in 2012 and 2013, then the M2 growth rate would only have only grown by 11.7 % and 12.2 %, respectively. Consequently, first, the pressure of excess supply could have been relieved to some extent; second, the growth of urban fixed assets investment would also have slowed down, dropping 2.5 and 2.3 percentage points respectively compared with actual values of the same year, which would have been conducive to relieve the pressure of government investment expansion for the purpose of economic growth, to improve the fiscal balance, to ease the burdens of government debts and to reduce corporate debt leverage ratio; third, the consumer price index would have dropped by 0.09 and 0.16 percentage points respectively; fourth, as to the gross demand structure, since the growth rate of investment would have slowed down, the gross capital formation ratio would have dropped by 0.20 and 0.33 percentage points, respectively. While residential consumption share to GDP would have increased by 0.07 and 0.08 percentage points respectively. Affected by the decline of import, the net export ratio

[7] Presumably, the trend of the US economy and the Euro-zone economy were not affected, and the interest rate, exchange rate and other variables remained the same as the actual values.

would have also increased by 0.06 and 0.09 percentage points. Generally, as the investment had declined, the gross demand structure therefore could have been improved slightly.

In addition, the simulation results also include:

1. If the economic growth target had been reduced to 7.2 %, the employment market would not have been worsened significantly. On one hand, because of the change of population age structure, the growth of new labor force slowed down. On the other hand, the expansion of service industry would have provided more employment opportunity. In spite of the benefits to the economic structure, the employment opportunities would have decreased by merely 167,100 and 167,300 in 2012 and 2013, respectively. The loss of job positions could have been partially offset by the expansion of the service industry. Since job-to-applicant ratio was about 1.11, lowering the economic growth goals to around 7.2 % would not have produced obviously employment problems.
2. With a lower economic growth target, the government debt burdens could have been relaxed.[8]
3. Now, the domestic economy is experiencing a transition period in economic growth rate; painful period of structural adjustment; Preliminary adaptation stage of stimulating policies, and thus Chinese must change their lives with positive attitudes to adapt to an economy of the "new normal".

The simulation gives us important implications. If the economic growth target were reduced to a lower level, the government could use micro-stimulus policies less frequently for the purpose of stable growth, and the government could concentrate on deepening reform, adjusting economic structure and transferring development modes. Therefore, the potential economic growth rate will be promoted, and the prospective of China's economy will be bright.

---

[8] If keeping the annual average economic growth rate at 7.1 % during the 13th Five-Year Plan period (from 2015 to 2020), the general government debts balance will decrease 2.06 trillion CNY, which will definitely have positive effects on relieving the government debts pressure.

Chapter 2
A Review of China's Economy in the First Half of 2014

2.1 The Economic Growth Rate Continued to Slow Down, the Employment Increased in the Tertiary Industry

In the first half of 2014, the growth rate of gross domestic product (GDP) continued to fall in China. Compared to the same period of last year, the real GDP grew by 7.4 %, which was the lowest in the last 4 years. Specifically, real GDP grew by 7.4 % in the first quarter, and rose to 7.5 % in the second quarter owing to micro-stimulus policies. The major reasons for the slowdown of economic growth were the weak growth of investment in the manufacturing industries and real estate sector. The cumulative growth rate of total industrial added value was 8.8 %, the lowest level since 2010 (Fig. 2.1).

Although the economic growth continued to decline, the share of value-added output of the tertiary industry in GDP kept rising quickly. It reached 46.1 %, 2.2 percentage points (Fig. 2.2) higher compared to secondary industry in 2013, and it rose further to 46.6 % in the first half of 2014, 0.6 percentage points higher compared to the secondary industry. The expansion of the service or tertiary industry guaranteed a stable employment. For example, in 2013, an increase of one billion CNY output in the tertiary industry could create about 11,000 jobs, while the same output in the second industry would only create 9,000 jobs. Although the economic growth slowed down in the first quarter of 2014, the requirement rate remained 1.11 in the labor market.[1] To some extent, it indicated that the slowdown of current economic growth has not yet hindered the labor market.[2]

[1] The requirement of 1.11 means that the employer supplies 1.11 jobs for each job seeker in the labor market.

[2] Recently the impact of changes in the aging structure of China's population is also of concern. By the late of 2012, the working-age population aged 15–59 (including whose age was under 60) was 937 million, 3.45 million less than the last year; by the end of 2013, the working-age population decreased to 920 million further.

CMR of Xiamen University, *China's Macroeconomic Outlook*,
Current Chinese Economic Report Series, DOI 10.1007/978-3-662-45405-3_2

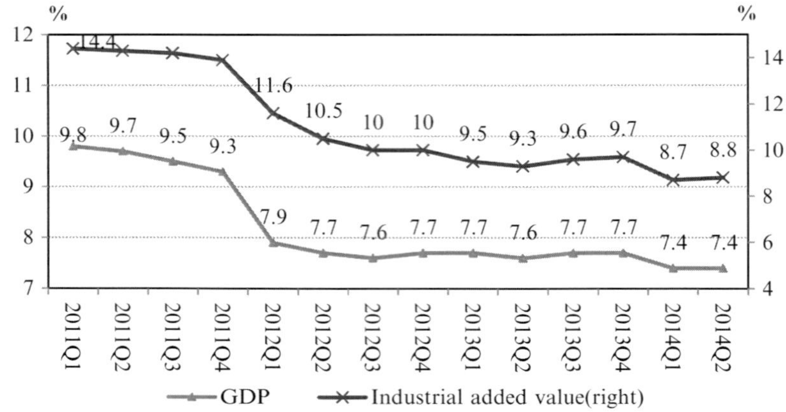

Fig. 2.1 The growth rates of real GDP and industrial added value, on the year-on-year basis (Data Source: CEIC Data)

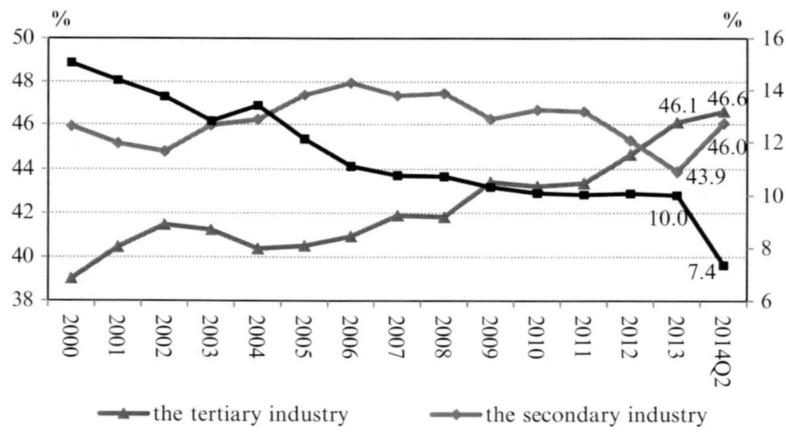

Fig. 2.2 The shares of value added output of three industries in GDP (Data Source: CEIC Data)

2.2 The Investment Growth Continued to Decline in the Fixed Assets, but Grew Fast in the Infrastructure Construction

In the first half of 2014, the cumulative growth of investment in fixed assets (excluding the investment of rural households) was 17.3 %, a decrease of 2.8 percentage points over the last year, mainly because of the decreasing growth of investment in the manufacturing industries and real estate industry. As a result of excess production capacity and weak recovery of demand from the external market in the first half year,

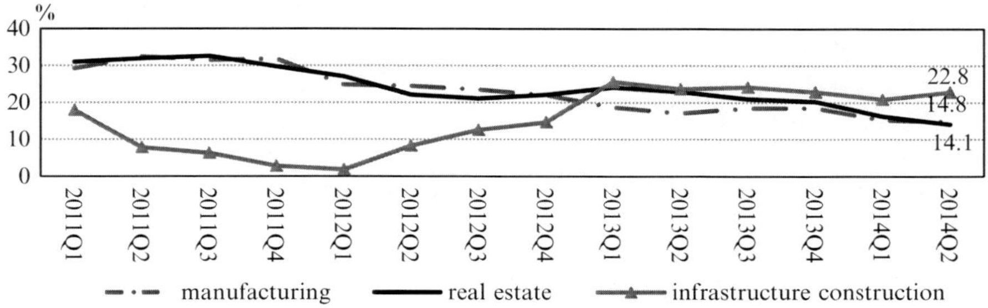

Fig. 2.3 The cumulative growth rate of nominal fixed asset investment in the main industries (Data Source: CEIC Data)

the cumulative growth rate of investment in manufacturing industries was only 14.8 %, a decrease of 2.3 percentage points over last year, which was also the lowest in the last decade. Besides, as the cool down of the real estate market, the growth of housing sales decreased and the housing inventory accumulated. A considerable number of cities experienced a sharp cut in the sales of the real estate,[3] which directly undermined the investment growth in the real estate industry. The cumulative growth of the real estate investment was 14.1 % in the first half of 2014, a decrease of 8.8 percentage points over last year. In fact, the rapid growth of the investment in the infrastructure construction had offset the adverse impact of weak investment in the manufacturing industries and real estate industry in the first half of 2014. The cumulative growth rate of investment in the infrastructure construction reached 22.8 %, an increase of 1.3 percentage points over the previous year (Fig. 2.3).[4] The improvement of infrastructure investment, to some extent, stopped a further decline of investment in the total fixed assets.

Compared the first half of 2014 with the same period of 2013, the cumulative growth of investment from the state-owned and state-holding enterprises, the private sector, Hong Kong, Macao and Taiwan enterprises, foreign enterprises was 14.8 %, 20.1 %, 4.8 % and 0.1 %, decreases of 2.7, 3.3, 2.7, 3.8 percentage points respectively. The substantial decrease of investment growth from the private sector and foreign enterprises was the major reason that led to a decline of investment growth in the total fixed assets. Moreover, viewed by the sources of projects, the investment growth from the central projects was 14.6 %, an increase of 4.9 percentage points over the previous year; the investment growth from the local government projects

[3] The average prices of new home in 100 cities fell more evidently in July, keeping a decreasing trend in the recent 3 months. Moreover, the price cut was more evident in the big ten cities, exceeding the average level in the country. Quoted from China Index Academy, "China Real Estate Index System and 100 city price index report in July", http://www.shenmou.com/caijing/201408/39535.html?news.baidu

[4] The infrastructure construction included the transportation, storage and postal services, water conservancy, environment and public facilities management industry as well as electricity, heat, gas and water production and supply industry.

was 17.5 %, a decrease of 3.2 percentage points over the last year. Thus, in order to maintain stable growth, a series of stimulus policies were implemented by the central government, especially viewed from the sources of investment projects. At present, the debt of local government is heavy, and 2014 will be the peak time for its debt payment. The local governments would not be able to implement micro-stimulus to maintain stable growth policies.[5] Finally, viewed from the funds source for investment, the growth rates of funds from the domestic loan, self-raised fund and foreign investment were 12.9, 16.7 and −8.3 %, which were basically just on the same level of the first half of 2013.

The investment growth is expected to keep declining in the second half of 2014, the main reasons are as follows:

1. It would take some time to cut the excess production capacity due to the high investment during past years.
2. The slump of real estate market since the first half of 2014 and the high inventory would directly undermine the recovery of investment growth in the real estate industry.[6]
3. The large amount of debt repayment, in the first half of 2014, would suppress the investment of the local governments. Furthermore, the huge inventory of the real estate would hinder the local governments from selling land. Hence, the expansion of investment by the local governments would be impossible due to less revenue from selling land..
4. Though a series of policies have been launched in order to promote private investment, the actual effects are quite uncertainty in the second half of 2014.

Therefore, we believe that the investment growth would continue to decline in the second half of 2014, and the slowdown of investment growth would undermine the economic growth in future.

2.3 The Growth of Trade Continued to Fall Significantly, the Increase of Trade Surplus Narrowed

In the first half of 2014, the exports grew 0.9 % (USD), a decrease of 9.5 percentage points over the same period of last year; the imports grew 1.5 %, a drop of 5.2 percentage points (Fig. 2.4). The trade surplus increased 102.9 billion USD, a decrease of 5.09 billion USD. The actual foreign direct investment rose to 2.2 %, an increase

[5] If the government could appropriately reduce the GDP growth target, complete the reforms to match financial power with office authority between the central and local government, regulate the bond financing of local government, it would allow the local governments to gradually get rid of the finance dependence on land.

[6] As the cut of inventory in the real estate is a slow process, although many provinces launched policy such as limitations on the home purchasing in order to stop home price from further falling, the expectation of price cut is difficult to change in the short term once such expectation was formed.

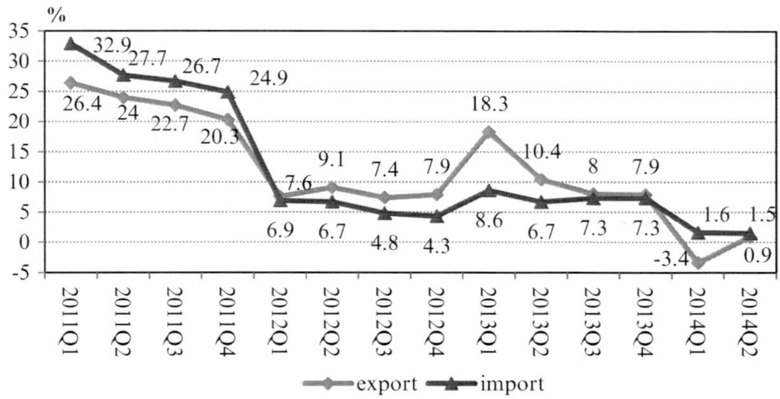

Fig. 2.4 The year-on-year growth of nominal exports and imports (Data Source: CEIC Data)

of 2.7 percentage points; the new foreign exchange reserves reached 169 billion USD, a drop of 8.7 percentage points. The main reason for the decline of export growth was the weak recovery of demand from the external market.[7] Specially, first, as the United State was affected by the cold snowy weather and its economic statistics were seasonally adjusted in the first quarter of 2014,[8] it led to a significant contraction of 2.9 % in its GDP growth; Second, the expectation of the exit of QE3 in the United States led to the substantial depreciation of currencies of emerging markets, which also had a negative impact on the exports of China. The decline in import growth was mainly due to the slowdown of domestic economic growth. However, beyond the cyclical factors, the domestic economic restructuring, the transformation of developing mode, the international economic rebalancing caused by the international financial crisis and new changes in the international economic environment perhaps were the further reasons that led to the slowdown of growth in exports or imports recently. As the adjustment of China's economic growth mode, the foreign trade will enter a new phase and the super high-speed growth of trade during 2002–2007 could not be reproduced and a lower growth rate in foreign trade will be achievable.[9]

[7] In addition, the true export of last year was "over-estimated" by the statistic authority.

[8] The bad weather in the winter had rather a negative impact on the consumption, fixed assets investment and trade in the United States during the first quarter of 2014. Specially, based on the substantial rise of inventory in the second half of 2013, the significant decrease of inventory brought about a decrease of 1.7 percentage points in GDP growth rate for the first quarter of 2014.

[9] Some scholars believe that, besides the GDP growths in the world and China, the proportion of China's exports accounted for the total exports in the world is an empirical observation data that can be used as basis for further projection. According to such estimates for the next decade, the reasonable range for China's trade growth rate should be 3–4 percentage points higher than the counterpart in the world, and China's growth rate of exports is probably 4–5 percentage points higher than the speed in the world. Quoted from Chang Hong Pei: "Building an open economy," "China Economic Herald", 2014, Number 14.

Turning to the trade composition, in the first half of 2014, the general trade exports grew 8.4 %, a drop of 1.6 percentage points over the same period of 2013; the general trade imports grew 6.2 %, an increase of 3.2 percentage points. The deficit of general trade accounted for 13.3 billion USD, 10 billion USD less than the last year. The growth of processing trade exports decreased 2 %, a decrease of 1.1 percentage points; the growth of processing trade imports fell 1.1 %, a drop of 5.7 percentage points. As a net effect, the surplus of processing trade narrowed to 167.4 billion USD.

In the first half of 2014, the exports to Association of Southeast Asian Nations (ASEAN) increased to 7.1 %, a drop of 15.6 percentage points over the previous year; the exports to European Union (EU) grew 9.9 %, nearly 14 percentage points more than the previous year; the exports to the United States of America (USA) increased 5.1 %, an increase of 3.4 percentage points over the previous year. On the import side, the imports from ASEAN grew 2.2 %, an increase of 0.5 percentage points; the imports from EU grew 16.2 %, an increase of 18.4 percentage points; the imports from USA grew 5.0 %, a drop of nearly 10 percentage points. By the end of the first half of 2014, the shares of exports in total to ASEAN, EU and USA were 11.6 %, 16.2 % and 16.7 % respectively, an increase of 0.7, 1.3 and 0.7 percentage points over the same period of previous year respectively; the shares of imports in total to ASEAN, EU and USA were 10.2 %, 12.4 % and 8.3 % respectively, an increase of 0.1, 1.6 and 0.3 percentage points over the first half of previous year respectively.

2.4 The Growth of Real Income Rebounded Slightly, the Growth of Total Retail Sales of Social Consumer Goods Kept Falling

In the first half of 2014, the per capita disposable income of urban residents was 14,959 CNY, a growth of 7.1 %. Although it was an increase of 0.6 percentage points of growth rate compared with the first half of 2013, it was a decrease of 2.6 percentage points compared with the same period of 2012.

The per capita cash income of rural residents was 5396 CNY, a growth of 9.8 % compared with the same period of 2013. Though it was an increase of 0.6 percentage points over the same period in 2013, it was a decrease of 2.6 percentage points compared with the same period in 2012 (Fig. 2.5). It shows that the decline in GDP growth in recent years has begun to suppress the growth of real income of urban or rural residents in China.

Due to the slowdown of growth of residential real income as well as the new restrictions on government consumption triggered by anti-corruption actions recently, the growth of the total retail sales of social consumer goods was directly restrained. In the first half of 2014, the total retail sales of social consumer goods grew by 12.1 %, a decrease of 0.6 percentage points over the same period of last year, which was also the lowest since 2008. Specially, according to the urban and

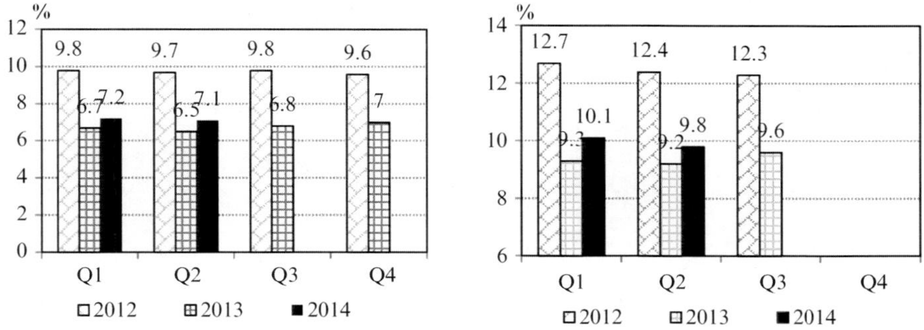

Fig. 2.5 The cumulative year-on-year real growth rates of urban per capita disposable income (*left*) and rural per capita cash income (*right*) (Data Source: CEIC) (Note: The National Bureau of Statistics does not publish the year-on-year real growth rate of the per capita cash income of rural residents at the end of the year)

rural areas, the retail sales of consumer goods in the urban area, which accounted for the 86 % in total, grew by 12.0 % that decreased by 0.5 percentage points compared with the first half of previous year; the retail sales in the rural area grew by 13.2 %, a decrease of 1.1 percentage points over the same period of last year.

2.5 CPI Maintained a Low Level, PPI Dropped More Slowly

At the end of June of 2014, the consumer price index (CPI) rose by 2.3 % over the same period of the previous year (Fig. 2.6), of which 65.2 % was contributed by the carryover effect, 34.8 % by the current price factors. The core CPI (excluding food and energy) and non-food CPI both rose by 1.7 %. The producer price index (PPI) is still negative but declined more and more slowly. In June, the PPI fell by 1.1 % compared with the same period of last year. On one hand, the long-lasting decline in PPI indicated the excess production capacity in the mining industry and some downstream manufacturing industries; On the other hand, the more and more slow decline of PPI means that the serious excess production capacity is gradually resolved.

2.6 Monetary Policy Was Targeted Easing; The Fiscal Policy Was Proactive and Prudent

In the first half of 2014, the People's Bank of China (PBC) continued its sound monetary policy, maintained the monetary aggregates at stable levels and optimized the structure. In the first quarter, the broad money (M2) rose by 12.1 %, 3.6 % lower

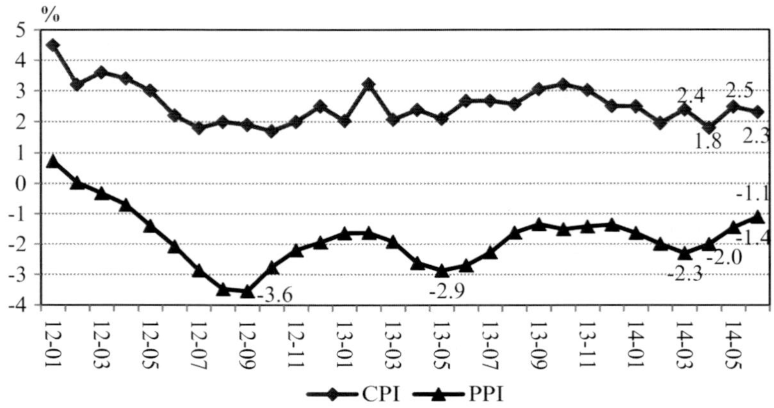

Fig. 2.6 The monthly year-on-year growth rates of the consumer price index (CPI) and the industrial producer price index (PPI) (Data Source: CEIC Data)

than last year. However, because of the targeted easing monetary policy[10] aiming at relieving downward pressure on economic growth in the next quarter, M2 rose by 14.7 % in the second quarter, 0.7 % higher than the same period of last year, and also exceed the 13 % target set by the PBC earlier this year. Therefore, the monetary policy is quite expansionary.

In the first half of 2014, RMB loans increased 5.74 trillion CNY, 659 billion CNY more than the same period of last year. Each month had almost 1 trillion of new CNY loans on average. Meanwhile, total social financing funds expanded rapidly to 10.57 trillion CNY, an increase of 414.6 billion CNY over the same period of previous year, also the highest since 2011 (Fig. 2.7). It is worth noting that while total social financing funds rose from 7.76 trillion CNY in 2011 to 10.57 CNY trillion in 2014, but the real GDP growth rate decreased from 9.6 to 7.4 % during the same period. It implies that the efficiency of investment has been deteriorated, which also means that investment-GDP ratio is increasing.

On the other hand, due to the expansion of the M2, the interest rate of interbank market remained at a low and stable level (Fig. 2.8). However, the enterprises in the real economy still suffered from ever-increasing cost and limited access to financing. The deviation of the wholesale interest rate and retail interest rate indicated that

---

[10] In April, the PBC cut required reserve rate of deposit (RRR) for country-level rural commercial banks and rural cooperative banks; In June, this targeted reduction of RRR policy have been extended to finance company, financial leasing company, auto leasing company and commercial banks that have compiled with prudential requirements and have reached the required ratios in their lending to the agricultural sector, rural areas, farmers, or to small and micro enterprise. Meanwhile, the China Banking Regulatory Committee (CBRC) also slightly relaxed the legal ratio of loan to deposit for commercial banks.

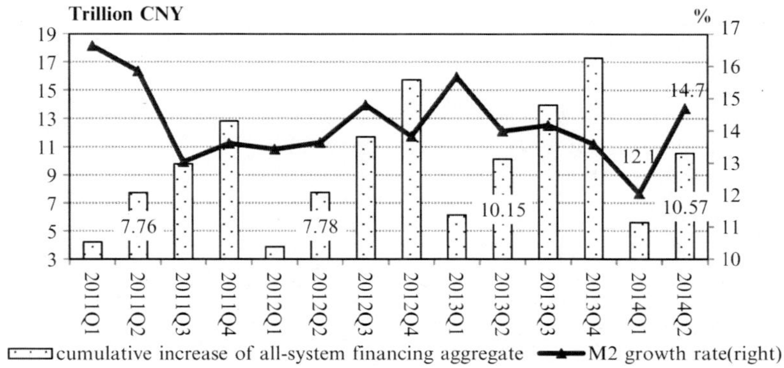

Fig. 2.7 The new incremental amount of total social financing funds and the growth rate of M2 (Data Source: CEIC Data)

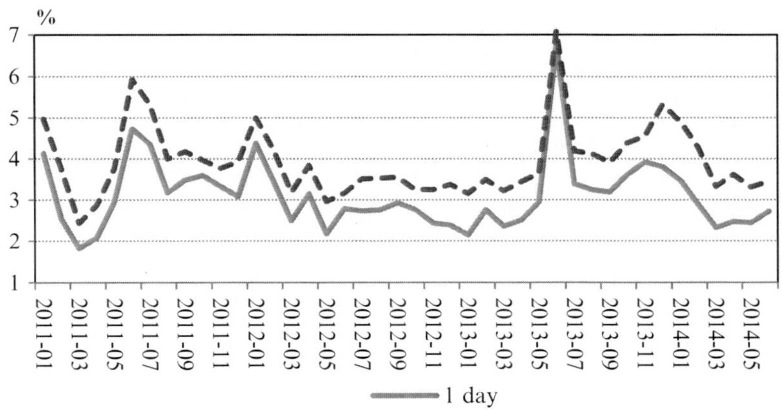

Fig. 2.8 The changes in the weighted average 1-day and 1-week interbank interest rate (Data source: CEIC Data)

the resource misallocation problem rooted deeply in the Chinese financial system, and the efficiency of funds allocation was still low in general.[11]

Moreover, the exchange rate of the CNY against the USD stopped appreciating on February 17 and depreciated dramatically thereafter.[12] On March 17, to build a two-way floating exchange rate regime that based on market supply and demand,

[11] There were other causes, including under development of the stock market and the high ratio of debt to asset for the enterprises.

[12] The depreciation can be largely explained by the ever-rising central parity of the CNY against the USD by the operations of PBC since Jan 14 of 2014. There are two purpose of PBC's action: first, to discourage the arbitrage behavior between the on shore and off shore CNY market; second, to set the stage for the widening of the floating band of the CNY exchange rate.

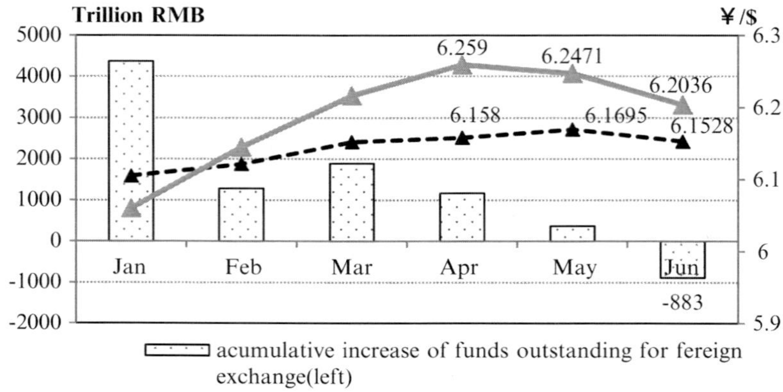

Fig. 2.9 The monthly cumulate increase of funds outstanding for foreign exchange, the spot market exchange rate and the central parity of the CNY against the USD (Data source: CEIC Data)

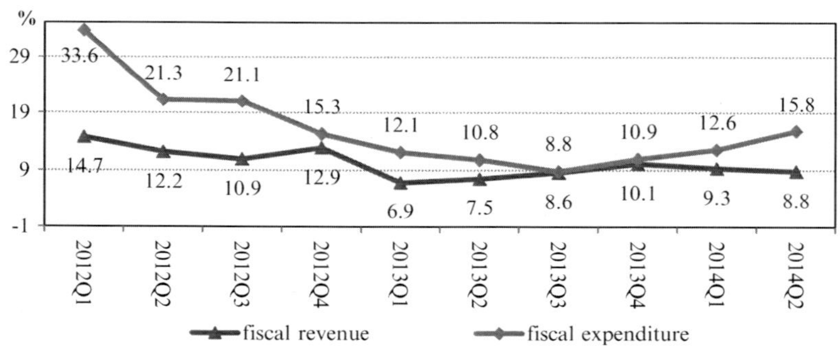

Fig. 2.10 The nominal growth rates of public fiscal revenue and expenditure (Data source: CEIC)

the PBC decided to enlarge the floating band of the exchange rate of the CNY against the USD on the interbank spot exchange rate market from 1 to 2 %. The CNY kept depreciating until June when it returned to the original rising track. At the end of June, the exchange rate of CNY reached 6.20 CNY per USD, up by 2.53 % since 2014. During this process, the funds outstanding for foreign exchange rose dramatically from January to April, and then gradually turn to negative in June whenever the funds outstanding for foreign exchange decreased by 88.3 billion (Fig. 2.9).

As to fiscal policy, the government fiscal revenue rose by 8.8 % in the first half of 2014, 1.3 % higher than the same period of last year (Fig. 2.10). Specifically, the tax revenue rose by 8.5 %, 0.6 % higher than the last year; the non-tax revenue rose by 11.1 %, 5.8 % higher than the last year. Although the growth rate of government fiscal revenue has decreased since 2014, the growth rate of government fiscal

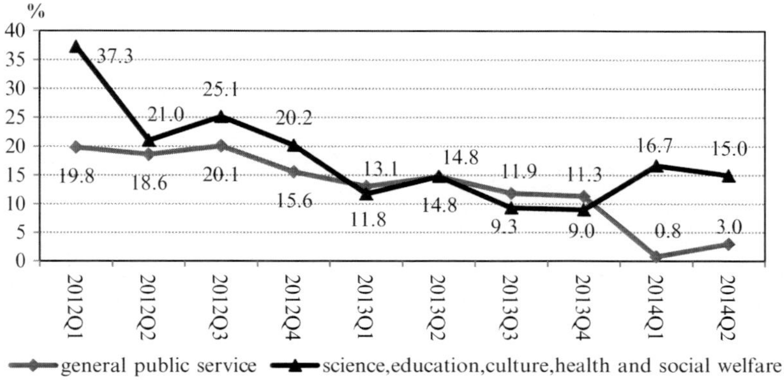

Fig. 2.11 The nominal growth rates of government expenditure by items (Data source: CEIC Data)

expenditure accelerated significantly (Fig. 2.10) whose accumulated growth rate reached 15.8 % at the end of June of 2014, 5 % higher than the same period of last year. As a net effect, the expenditure grew 7 percentage points faster than the revenue.

From late March, the State Council initiated series of micro-stimulus packages, including the tax cut for small and micro enterprises, rebuilding of rundown urban areas, the railway construction in the middle and western parts of China, financial support to the agricultural sector, rural areas, and farmers, promotion of exports, improvement of employment, acceleration of water conservancy project constructions, etc. Among the fiscal expenditure, the general public service expenditure rose by 3.0 % and accounted for 8.6 % in total expenditure in the first half of 2014, 11.8 and 1.8 % lower than the same period of last year respectively. The expenditure of science, education, culture, health and social welfare rose by 15.0 % and accounted for 38.3 % in total expenditure in the first half of 2014, 0.2 % higher and 0.2 % lower than the same period of last year respectively (Fig. 2.11). On the other hand, the expenditure of infrastructure construction and government-subsidized housing rose dramatically. Among them, the transportation expenditure rose by 22.1 % and accounted for 6.37 % in total expenditure in the first half year, 24.5 and 0.33 % higher than the first half of last year respectively. The agriculture supporting expenditure rose by 17.6 % and accounted for 8.74 % in total expenditure in the first half year, 6.14 and 0.13 % higher than the first half of last year respectively. The government-subsidized housing expenditure rose by 30.2 % and accounted for 2.92 % in total expenditure in the first half of 2014, 34.5 and 0.32 % higher than the first half of 2013 respectively.

In Conclusion, the Chinese GDP growth rate has decreased gradually since the global financial crisis, from 14.2 % in 2007, dramatically dropped to 9–10 % during 2008–2011, dropped to 7.7 % in 2012, and then dropped further in 2013.

In the first half of 2014, the real GDP growth rate dropped slightly to 7.4 %. The main reasons include: (1) The investment growth dropped dramatically. Specifically, the investment and output of manufacturing industries grew slowly due to the excess production capacity problem accumulated during decades. Moreover, the growth of investment in real estate decreased even more significantly due to the stagnant sales and high level of inventory. (2) The decreasing growth of net export was the result of the slow recovery of the global economy. (3) The domestic consumption demand was still weak: the growth of retail sales of social consumer goods was slow, the growth of real income of residents was not significant and the government spending on official overseas visits, official vehicles, and official hospitality was curbed.

Due to the stagnation of residential income, the efficiency of the micro-stimulus and targeted easing policies still has to rely on the investment in infrastructure construction to maintain stable growth. In the last 3 years, the micro-stimulus policies mainly focused on two areas: (1) the infrastructure construction such as railway, public facilities and water conservancy projects; (2) the construction of government-subsidized housing and reconstruction of rundown urban areas. However, as the monetary supply as well as all-system financing aggregate continued to expand rapidly, the marginal effect of the investment on promoting economic growth was diminishing Therefore, China's economy still relies heavily on the investment, a situation hard to change fundamentally.

It take time to fix the problem of the excess production capacity. Therefore, the local governments who suffer large amount of debts would be not able to start a new round of large-scale investment projects. Meanwhile, although packages of stimulus measures aiming at supporting the private investment have been introduced since earlier of this year, the efficiency of these measures is still unclear. As a result, the investment growth would continue to decline inevitably in the second half of 2014.

It would merely be a huge waste of social resource through investment of the government in order to maintain high economic growth. Thus, the central government should realize that Chinese economic growth had entered a new phase of development. The domestic economy is experiencing a transition period in economic growth rate; painful period of structural adjustment; preliminary adaptation stage of stimulating policies, and thus Chinese is changing their lives with positive attitudes to adapt to an economy of "new normal". The central government should avoid setting an economic growth target as high as before. In our opinion, the labor market and employment should remain robust if the growth target is properly reduced and the government could take advantage of the adjustment of industrial structure. Moreover, the government should take advantage of "the new normal", and concentrate on deepening reform, correcting the distorted financial system, and transforming the developing mode.

Chapter 3
Forecast of China's Economy for 2014–2015

3.1 Assumptions of Exogenous Variables

3.1.1 Economic Growth Rates of the United States and the Euro-zone

In 2014, due to the weather and seasonal adjustment factors,[1] the US economy uncommonly shrank 2.9 % in the first quarter. However, since then, some economic variables from the United States, such as employees on nonfarm payrolls, retail sales, core durable goods orders, privately-owned housing starts, housing sales, new applications for unemployment benefits, auto sales and manufacturing, have been improved significantly. The US economy grew 4 % in the second quarter, and is expected to be more than 3 % in the third and fourth quarter. On July 14, the IMF forecast that the growth rate of the US economy will be 1.7 % in 2014, and will rise to 3 % in 2015.

Turning to the Euro-zone, the economy has been recovering gradually for five consecutive quarters. Meanwhile, financial market conditions have been improving significantly. IMF forecasts that the economy will grow 1.08 % and 1.5 % in 2014 and 2015, respectively (Fig. 3.1).

---

[1] Severe weather in winter caused serious impacts on consumption, fixed investment and trade, and the significant decline in inventories in the first quarter of 2014 also brought a drag of 1.7 percentage points to GDP after the sharp rise in inventories in the third quarter and fourth quarter of 2013.

CMR of Xiamen University, *China's Macroeconomic Outlook*,
Current Chinese Economic Report Series, DOI 10.1007/978-3-662-45405-3_3

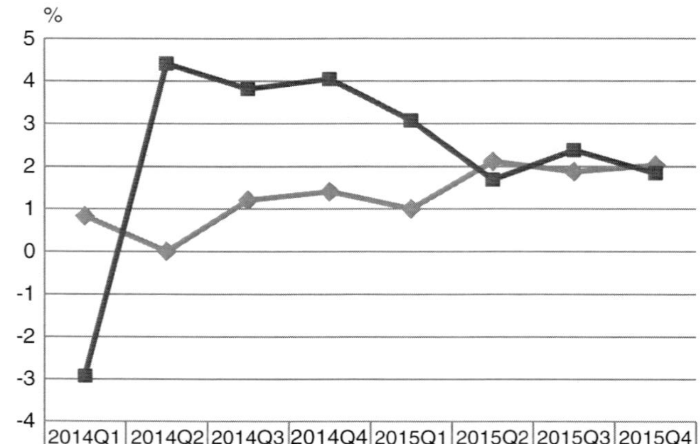

	2014Q1	2014Q2	2014Q3	2014Q4	2015Q1	2015Q2	2015Q3	2015Q4
EU17GDP_C	0.83	0.00	1.21	1.41	1.00	2.12	1.88	2.03
USGDP_C	-2.93	4.41	3.81	4.04	3.07	1.69	2.38	1.84

Fig. 3.1 Assumptions of growth in the United States and the Euro-zone (Note: "EU17GDP_C" denotes growth rate of the Euro-zone, while "USGDP_C" denotes that of the United States)

3.1.2 Major Exchange Rates

In 2014, the exchange rate trend suddenly reversed. The unilateral appreciation era has ended with slight depreciation of CNY against USD after February. Compared with the beginning of the year, the central parity rate has depreciated 0.9 %, and the spot exchange rate has depreciated 2.53 % in the end of June.

In the first half year, with the recovery of the external demand and the loose domestic monetary policy, China's economic growth stop declining, but the depreciation trend of CNY is still weak.

In the second half of 2104, domestic demand is expected to remain weak; but the economies of the major trading partners of China such as the US, the Euro-zone will keep improving, so that China will continue to maintain a certain scale of trade surplus. In addition, China is not likely to significantly relax capital controls in the short term, the current account and financial capital account of China will remain in surplus. More importantly, the possibility of a large scale outflow of capital is low because investment return in China is high. Therefore, in the next 2 years, the possibility of the substantial depreciation of the CNY is not expected. The appreciation of the CNY may revive modestly in the second half of 2014. The exchange rate of the USD against the CNY will be about 1:6.14 until the end of the third quarter, and 1:6.12 until the end of the fourth quarter.

In 2015, the CNY is likely to rise slightly because the external demand will keep improving. The exchange rate of the USD against the CNY is expected to slightly rise by 0.3 % for the whole year. There might be a slight depreciation followed by

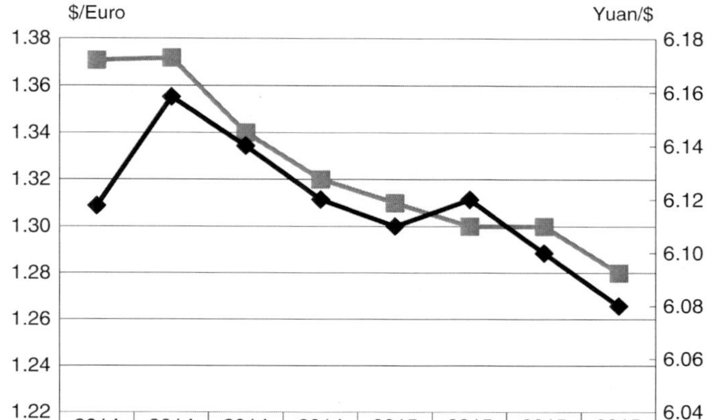

	2014 Q1	2014 Q2	2014 Q3	2014 Q4	2015 Q1	2015 Q2	2015 Q3	2015 Q4
USDEURO	1.37	1.37	1.34	1.32	1.31	1.30	1.30	1.28
ER_W	6.12	6.16	6.14	6.12	6.11	6.12	6.10	6.08

Fig. 3.2 Assumptions of major exchange rates (Note: "ER_W" denotes the exchange rate of the CNY against the USD, and "USDEURO" denotes that of the USD against the EUR)

slight appreciation due to interest rate hikes in U.S. in the second quarter, the exchange rate of the USD against the CNY will be about 1:6.08 until the fourth quarter (Fig. 3.2).

Although the economy of the Euro-zone is improving, the recovery is not strong enough due to the lack of market demand, the low price level, the insufficiency of investment demand, the heavy debt and the high unemployment in some countries. The structural conflict between capital, labor and product markets hindered the rebalancing of investment and financing, and the improvement of productivity. In June 2014, the initial annualized inflation rate in the Euro-zone is 0.5 %, the same as last month, the lowest point in last 4 years. For a long period of time, the inflation rate will be lower than 2 %, the warning line set by the European Central Bank for the sake of price stability. Hence, the Euro-zone will face the risk of deflation. Therefore, in early June, the European Central Bank announced loose monetary policy, such as cutting interest rates, so that the Euro-zone entered the era of negative interest rates for the first time. Presumably, the European Central Bank will adopt more loose monetary policies in the future in order to enhance liquidity, to drive the inflation rate back to around 2 %.

Meanwhile, the US job market keeps improving, and the inflation rate begins to approach the target value (2.0 %). The Federal Reserve will continue to reduce the scale of the purchase of treasury bonds, and is expected to end QE in October, 2014 and to raise interest rates in 2015, which will be the first rate increase after the global financial crisis, and will boost the dollar index to a large extent. With this background, the EUR will plunge against the USD, and the exchange rate of the EUR against the USD at the end of 2014 will be 1:1.32 and 1:1.28 in 2015.

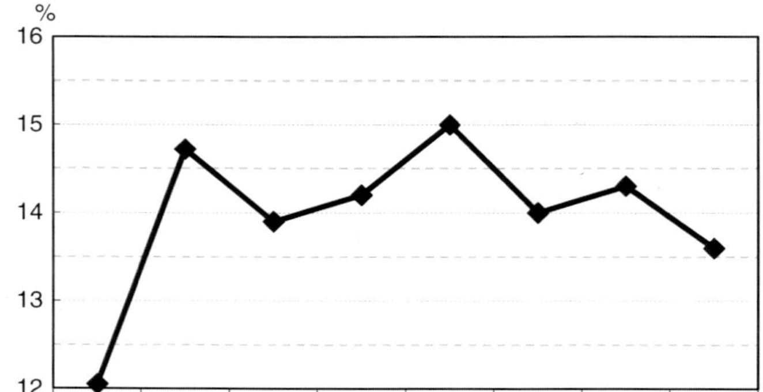

	2014 Q1	2014 Q2	2014 Q3	2014 Q4	2015 Q1	2015 Q2	2015 Q3	2015 Q4
M2	12.1	14.7	13.9	14.2	15.0	14.0	14.3	13.6

Fig. 3.3 Assumptions of the growth rate of M2

3.1.3 The Growth Rate of Broad Money Supply (M2)

In the first half of 2014, the central bank implemented twice the policies of targeted reserve ratio cut to relieve the downward pressure of economic growth. The overall credit conditions are loose, and the year-on-year growth of M2 reaches 14.7 %. Economic growth, inflation, and liquidity have created good conditions for loose monetary policy.[2] The growth rate of M2 will be about 14.2 % at the end of 2014. The commercial loans will increase fast and then slowdown, and the new RMB loan for the whole year of 2014 is expected to reach ten trillion CNY, higher than the previous year.

In 2015, with the improvement of external environment, expansion of exports and the less downward pressure on economic growth, the growth rate of M2 will fall to 13.6 %, slightly slower than the previous year (Fig. 3.3).[3]

[2] In the second half, the goals of monetary policy are expected be: maintaining economic growth stably and optimizing economic structure. First, the central bank is expected to intensify directional loose, to increase support to key areas and weak areas, such as small and micro businesses, agriculture, rural areas and farmers and the shantytown improvement project. Second, the central bank is expected to continue to release liquidity: to guide to credit and improve the central bank collateral management framework, to expand the channels of base money, to elongate delivery deadline, thereby reducing the social financing cost and stabilizing business expectations. In addition, a loosening credit policy is expected in the second half.

[3] The prudent monetary policy should focus on reducing capital costs in the long run, and moderately lowering the deposit reserve ratio and interest rates. If economy is worsening in the third and fourth quarter of 2014, the monetary policy may enhance a loose policy, and interest rates ma y be cut by 25 basis points in the fourth quarter.

3.2 Forecasts of China's Major Macroeconomic Indicators for 2014–2015

3.2.1 *Growth Rate of GDP*

Based on the assumptions of exogenous variables made above, the CQMM predicts that, China's economic growth rate will continue to fall slightly to 7.49 % in 2014, a decrease of 0.21 percentage points compared with previous year, and it will further fall to 7.37 % in 2015. The main reasons are: first, the final consumption will be restricted by the declining growth rate of residential income; second, the marginal efficiency of the investment on GDP is diminishing; third, the growth rate of export will be constrained by the increasing labor cost and the slight appreciation of the RMB.

The GDP growth rate will remain stable. It will drop to 7.42 % in the third quarter of 2014 compared with the previous year, and then rise slightly to 7.62 % in the fourth quarter, due to the decline of investment in the real estate sector, the weakness of external demand in the near future.

The quarterly growth trend of 2015 will be the same as that of 2014—from low to high (Fig. 3.4).

3.2.2 *Major Price Indices*

3.2.2.1 The CPI

The CQMM predicts that, the CPI will reach 2.51 % in 2014, a decrease of 0.12 % percentage points over the previous year, and rise to 2.80 % in 2015.

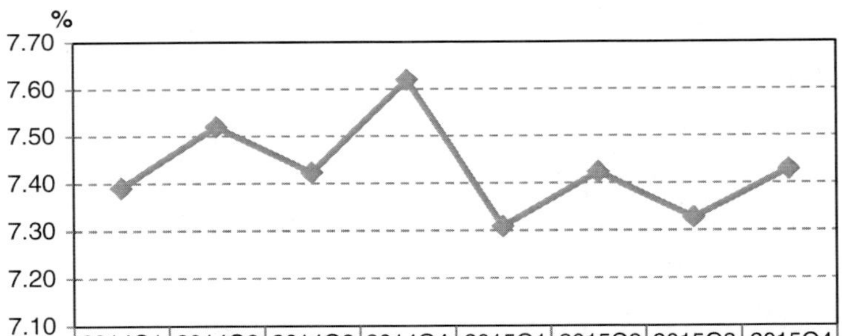

	2014Q1	2014Q2	2014Q3	2014Q4	2015Q1	2015Q2	2015Q3	2015Q4
GDP	7.39	7.52	7.42	7.62	7.31	7.42	7.33	7.43

Fig. 3.4 Forecast of GDP quarterly growth rate (year-on-year basis)

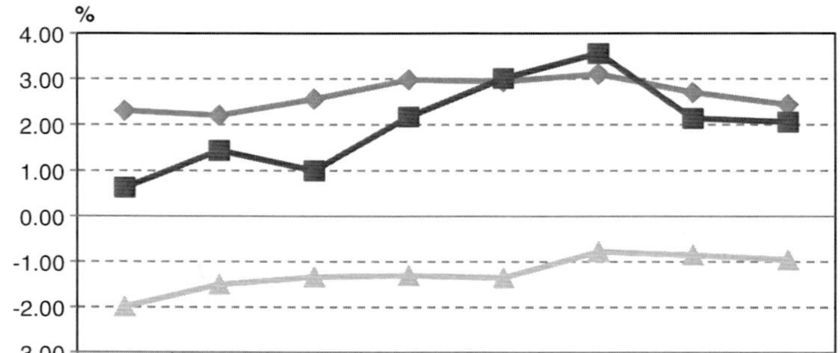

	2014Q1	2014Q2	2014Q3	2014Q4	2015Q1	2015Q2	2015Q3	2015Q4
CPI	2.31	2.20	2.56	2.98	2.94	3.11	2.70	2.44
PPI	-1.99	-1.50	-1.33	-1.31	-1.35	-0.78	-0.85	-0.95
P_GDP	0.63	1.44	1.00	2.17	3.01	3.56	2.14	2.06

Fig. 3.5 Forecasts of major price indices (year-on-year basis) (Note: CPI, "P_GDP", and PPI denote consumer price index, GDP deflator, and producer price index, respectively)

Quarter by quarter (Fig. 3.5), CPI may rise to 2.56 % in the third quarter of 2014, and then rise to 2.98 % in the fourth quarter. In 2015, CPI is forecast to reach 2.94 % in the first quarter, then reach a peak of 3.11 % in the second quarter and finally fall to 2.44 % in the fourth quarter.

3.2.2.2 The PPI

The PPI in the next 2 years will remain negative, but it will decline more and more slowly. The PPI is expected to be −1.53 % and −0.98 % in 2014, and in 2015, respective.

Quarter by quarter (Fig. 3.5), the PPI is forecast to rise to −1.31 % in the fourth quarter of 2014. In 2015, the PPI is forecast to rise to −0.78 % in the second quarter and then decrease to −0.95 % in the fourth quarter.

3.2.2.3 The GDP Deflator

The GDP deflator (P_GDP) is expected to rise to 1.31 % and 2.69 % in 2014 and 2015, respectively.

Examined quarter by quarter, P_GDP will fall to 1.00 % in the third quarter of 2014 and then pick up gradually to its peak at 3.56 % in the second quarter of 2015. It will fall through the third quarter and then go down to 2.06 % in the fourth quarter of 2015 (Fig. 3.5).

To sum up, the economic growth will continue to slow down in the second half of 2014, and the GDP growth rate is expected to be 7.49 % in 2014. Annual inflation is expected to remain moderate, and the CPI is expected to rise to 2.51 %. Due to excess production capacity of manufacturing industry increase in the inventory of real estate industries and the pressure of paying debt of local governments, the economic growth will slow down gradually. However, because the growth of M2 will exceed 14 %, much higher than the target set in the beginning of the year, the CPI will rise to 2.80 % in 2015.

3.2.3 Forecasts of Growth Rates of Other Major Macroeconomic Indicators

3.2.3.1 Export, Import, and Foreign Exchange Reserve Growth

The Model predicts that in 2014, due to the accelerating recovery of the US economy and the alleviation of uncertainty of economies of the Euro-zone, China's import and export growths will restore. Calculated in USD, total exports are expected to grow by 5.15 % in 2014, a decrease of 2.97 percentage points over the previous year. Total import growth is likely to fall to 5.52 %, a decrease of 1.71 percentage points over the previous year (Table 3.1). The growth of exports is expected to reach the peak of 11.78 % in the third quarter of 2014, and then decline to 8.93 % in the fourth quarter. The import is forecast to increase in the second half of 2014, reaching the peak of 8.59 % in the fourth quarter. As a result, the foreign exchange reserve (FER) is expected to rise by 12.75 % in 2014.

In 2015, the external demand is expected to be stable. The export, import and foreign exchange reserve, are forecast to grow at 10.23 %, 9.66 %, and 9.58 %, respectively (Table 3.1, Fig. 3.6).

3.2.3.2 Growth Rate of Total Fixed Assets

In 2014, due to the shrink of investment in real estate sector, urban fixed assets investment growth will be 17.12 %,[4] a decline of 2.57 % over precious year (Fig. 3.7). In 2015, affected by a new round of urbanization, urban investment demand will further increase. Consequently, the urban fixed assets investment growth will be 16.58 %.

Examined quarter by quarter, in 2014, urban fixed assets investment growth will fall to 16.68 % in the third quarter and then rise to 17.40 % in the fourth quarter. In 2015, the growth rate will fall in the first quarter, and then climbs up in the second and third quarter, and stay stable in the fourth quarter.

[4] Calculated at the current price.

Table 3.1 Forecast of the growth rates of exports and imports in 2014–2015 (%)

Time	Exports				Imports				Foreign exchange reserves
	RMB at constant price	USD	USD (general trade)	USD (processing trade)	RMB at constant price	USD	USD (general trade)	USD (processing trade)	USD (100 millions)
2014	5.30	5.15	9.68	4.00	4.85	5.52	8.27	4.84	12.75
Q1	−4.37	−3.55	6.20	−4.83	4.63	1.94	12.61	−6.37	14.56
Q2	6.52	4.87	10.22	0.73	0.41	1.51	0.80	4.54	14.15
Q3	11.78	11.84	12.98	11.16	5.68	7.47	6.55	12.48	12.51
Q4	7.93	7.93	9.32	9.13	8.59	10.91	13.15	9.04	10.07
2015	9.24	10.23	10.23	10.67	9.08	9.66	12.53	7.35	9.58
Q1	9.90	9.88	9.13	13.39	7.29	8.18	7.19	12.48	9.91
Q2	10.66	12.70	10.43	16.35	13.32	14.87	20.79	11.46	10.15
Q3	8.08	9.31	10.70	7.01	8.38	8.52	12.54	3.07	9.31
Q4	8.45	9.18	10.59	6.85	7.60	7.48	10.32	3.48	8.99

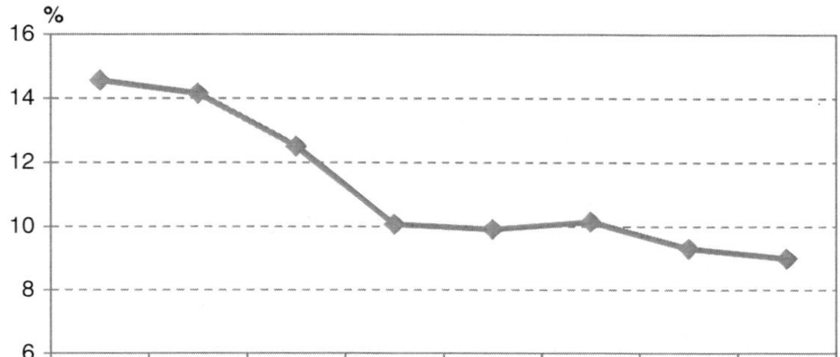

	2014Q1	2014Q2	2014Q3	2014Q4	2015Q1	2015Q2	2015Q3	2015Q4
FER	14.56	14.15	12.51	10.07	9.91	10.15	9.31	8.99

Fig. 3.6 Forecast of growth rate of foreign exchange reserves in 2014–2015 (year-on-year basis)

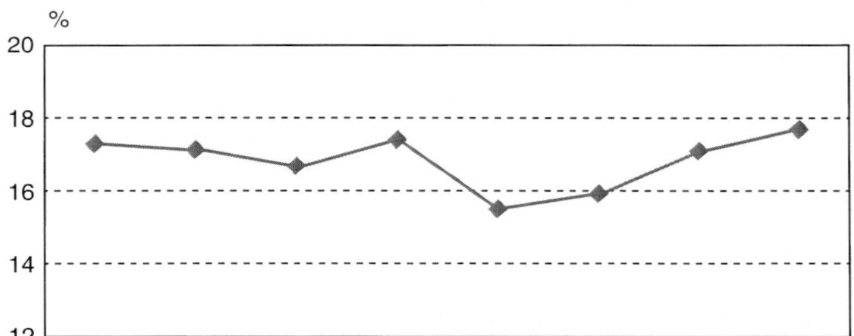

	2014Q1	2014Q2	2014Q3	2014Q4	2015Q1	2015Q2	2015Q3	2015Q4
FII	17.28	17.13	16.68	17.4	15.5	15.89	17.07	17.71

Fig. 3.7 Growth rate of total fixed assets formation (year-on-year basis) (Note: "FII" denotes the growth rate of fixed assets formation in urban areas at current price)

3.2.3.3 Growth Rate of Consumption

In 2014, the CQMM predicts that residential consumption will grow by 7.33 %, a drop of 0.13 % over the previous year. It will increase to 8.08 % in 2015.

In 2014, total retail sales of social consumer goods will grow by 12.61 %,[5] a drop of 0.35 % over the previous year, and will rise slightly to 14.12 % in 2015.

Quarter by quarter, the growth in total residential consumption[6] will rebound to 6.73 % in the third quarter of 2014, and pick up to 7.99 % in the fourth quarter.

However, there will be a big fluctuation in the growth of the residential consumption in 2015. It will drop to 6.28 % in the first quarter; reach the annual peak of 11.59 % in the second quarter, and then go down to 7.14 % in the fourth quarter.

[5] Calculated at the current price.

[6] Calculated at the current price.

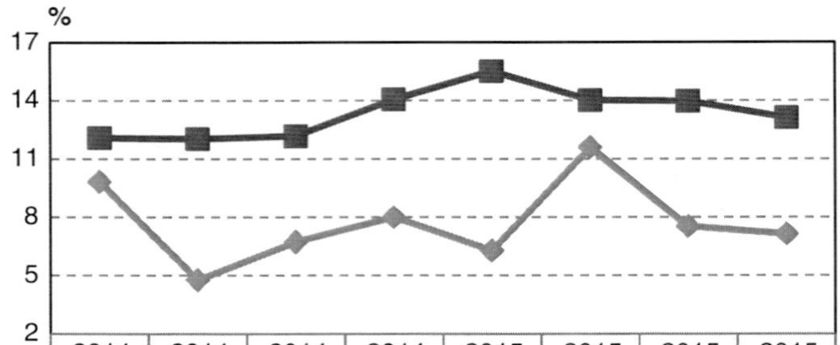

	2014 Q1	2014 Q2	2014 Q3	2014 Q4	2015 Q1	2015 Q2	2015 Q3	2015 Q4
CON_D_C	9.83	4.77	6.73	7.99	6.28	11.59	7.53	7.14
RETALL	12.09	12.04	12.18	14.05	15.51	14.01	13.97	13.12

Fig. 3.8 Growth rate of consumption (year-on-year basis) (Note: "CON_D_C" denotes the growth rate of residents' consumption and "RETAIL" denotes the growth rate of retail sales of total consumer goods at current price)

The growth in total retail sales of social consumer goods[7] will increase gradually in the second half of 2014. In 2015, it will fall relatively steadily quarter after quarter until it hits 13.12 % in the fourth quarter (Fig. 3.8).

In conclusion, even though the external demand will continue to rebound and money supply will continue to increase, the economic growth still tend to slow down. The economy is forecast to grow by 7.49 % in 2014, which means that the growth target of 7.5 % set by the Central Government will be achievable. And in 2015, the economic growth will fall gradually to 7.37 %. That means under the present growth pattern, the effect of micro-stimulus policy on relieving the downward pressure to maintain stable growth is diminishing.

At present, the micro-stimulus policies aiming at stable growth heavily relies on investment expansion. However, as predicted by the model, the growth rate for the urban investment in fixed assets[8] would be unlikely to increase in 2014, and maybe go down to 17.12 %, a decline of 2.57 % over previous year. In 2015, the growth rate of urban investment in fixed assets is forecast to be only 16.58 %. The reason that the micro-stimulus policy can't produce significant effect on expanding investment is as follows: The choice of private capital investment is limited compared to the SOEs, and private investment is mainly concentrated on the two fields: in manufacturing industries (accounted for 35 % of investment in fixed assets) and real estate (25 %). But manufacturing industries are experiencing excess production capacity and real estate sector are with increasing pressure of inventory. Therefore, the private capital is difficult to find good investment opportunities, and the private investment will slump.

[7] Calculated at the current price.

[8] Calculated at the current price.

On one hand, the purpose of micro-stimulus policy is "to achieve a great with doing little" or "use a small financial fund to simulate a lot of investment of the market players (excluding governments)". On the other hand, in order to maintain stable growth, the government turns out to be the key market player of investment, and the government intervention will reduce the efficiency of the investment and put a downward pressure on the contribution of investment to the GDP.

As predicted by CQMM, there is no big upward pressure on inflation rate, and CPI is expected to rise only to 2.51 % in 2014, a small drop over the previous year.

In 2015, if the central government insists on applying the micro-stimulus and targeted easing policies, the economic growth will continue to slow down, and CPI would pick up to 2.80 %, which will squeeze the space of using micro-stimulus policies further, constrain the growth of residential income, and the inflation rate will go up.

In 2014, the total retail sale of consumer goods[9] is forecast to grow at 12.61 %, a drop of 0.35 % over the previous year. And as wages rise and CNY appreciates, the growth rate of export will slow down. Total export[10] is expected to grow by 5.15 %, a decrease of 2.97 percentage points over the previous year. Total import growth is likely to fall to 4.85 %, a decrease of 2.39 percentage points over the previous year.

[9] Calculated at the current price.

[10] Calculated at current USD.

Chapter 4
Policy Simulations

In the first half of 2014, China's economic growth slowed down. To some extent, the decline of economic growth is a fragment of the downward phase of the economic cycle. Therefore, in order to better understand the economic trend in the first half year, we need to observe it from the very beginning.

The 4 trillion anti-crisis stimulus package launched by the former government in 2008 could not change fundamentally the economic development mode. Now with the exiting of the massive stimulus package, China is facing with great downward pressure of economic growth, which can also be attributed to many reasons. They are: slow recovery of international economies, the structural imbalances in domestic economy, the difficulty in civil system reform, the gradually shifting of driving force of the growth from manufacturing industries to service sector.

GDP growth rate kept declining during 2010–2012, from an annualized growth of 11.9 % in the first quarter of 2010 to 7.4 % in the third quarter of 2012, which even was lower than the economic growth target of the central government.[1]

In order to prevent economic growth from further declining, the new government implemented the policies for stable growth. Compared with previous government, the new government no longer adopted a one-time massive investment stimulus plan, but instead of a series of micro-stimulus policies to stabilize economic growth, mainly including that: releasing a number of railway, highway, municipal, energy, environmental protection and other infrastructure investment projects, encouraging private capital to participate in construction of government-subsidized housing, supporting micro or small enterprises development, accelerating the development of service industry, and promoting the stable growth of foreign trade, and so on.

Although these micro-stimulus policies help the economic growth rebound to 7.9 % in the fourth quarter of 2012, the target of stable economic growth wasn't fully achieved.

---

[1] During 2005–2011, about 7 years, the government expected annual economic growth rate was identified as 8 %. In March 2012, the expected economic growth was down to 7.5 % in "Government Work Report".

CMR of Xiamen University, *China's Macroeconomic Outlook*,
Current Chinese Economic Report Series, DOI 10.1007/978-3-662-45405-3_4

In 2013, the economic growth rate immediately fell to 7.6 % in the first quarter, and then further declined to 7.5 % in the second quarter. In order to prevent a further decline, with a new round of micro-stimulus policies the economic growth slightly rebounded to 7.8 % in the third quarter.

However, in 2014, a similar situation happened again. When the economic growth rate fell to a new lowest point: 7.4 %, a new round of the micro-stimulus policies was implemented in the second quarter. Though the policies were essentially the same as that of 2013, the economic growth rebounded only by 0.1 percentage points.

The macroeconomic performance in the past 3 years implies the following findings: (1) For each year, there existed a cyclical economic growth pattern: "decline—micro-stimulus—rebound—decline", and the length of the each cycle is becoming short year after year. (2) The micro-stimulus and targeted easing policies could only relieve the downward pressure of growth of infrastructure investment with very limited effect. In the past 3 years, the micro-stimulus and targeted easing policies mainly concentrated on infrastructure investment and government-subsidized housing: to launch infrastructure investment projects like railway, highway, municipality, energy, environmental protection and water conservancy, where private capital participation was encouraged; to boost the construction of government-subsidized housing, the reconstruction of the rundown urban areas. (3) For each year, the starting time of micro-stimulus policies had to be shifted to an earlier time, from the third quarter in 2012 to the middle of 2013, and then to the second quarter of 2014. (4) The effect of micro-stimulus policies on economy growth is diminishing. With the micro-stimulus policies, the growth rate increased by 0.5 percentage points in 2012, by 0.3 percentage points in 2013, and by only 0.1 percentage points in 2014.

Reviewing the results of macro-control policy since 2008 especially the past 3 years, we find the following implications:

1. International financial crisis has fundamentally changed the trend of China's economic growth, from constantly rising to constantly falling. The response measures (massive stimulus or micro-stimulus) not only couldn't reverse the declining tendency of growth, but further distorted the economic structure which had already been serious imbalance. Why this happens? Essentially, it is the result of the "investment-driven, export-led" growth mode formed in the past decades. The outbreak of international financial crisis has damaged the "export-led" engine of China's economic growth. Meanwhile, the decline in GDP growth after international financial crisis has inhibited the residential real income growth, though the residential real income had not kept pace with high growth of GDP before the crisis. Together with the low consume marginal propensity of residents, the "residential consumption" as growth engine was hard to have an effect on China's economy. Eventually, China had to rely on "investment-driven" to maintain stable growth. Although the 4-trillion massive stimulus package announced in 2008 had prevented the GDP growth from declining below 9 % during 2008–2012, it forced China's economic growth to rely on investment deeply further. Moreover, the excess production capacity of manufacturing

industries as well as the expansion of real estate inventory today is also one of the consequences the massive stimulus package. Not to mention the problem of corporate debt and government debt caused by the long-term credit binged in financial system. Since there was no major reform in economic system, economic development mode still remained unchanged and the economic structure further got into imbalance, when the 4 trillion investment plan gradually finished, the economic growth rate had sharply dropped to 8 % since 2012. Therefore, under the traditional growth pattern, the micro-stimulus policies are not the best choice, but China has no other choices. Such stimulus policies are basically the old idea of investment expansion. Once the recovery in external demand makes economic growth stable, the micro-stimulus policies need to exit.

2. In the long run, it is impossible for China to maintain the high-speed economic growth rate more than 8 % after international financial crisis, owing to the gross economic scale, the adjustment of population and industrial structure. And China will enter so-called the economy of "new normal", a middle-speed growth era However, in short-term, the uncertain external market, the domestic enterprises debt and local government debt as well as the high risk in financial system, are still factors to curb economic growth rate at a reasonable level. Using micro-stimulus policies to implement targeted control is not intended to pursue an artificial high growth rate target, but to shift smoothly into an economy of new normal. Meanwhile, the targeted reduction of deposit reserve ratio was used to adjust credit resources structure, to guide the capital inflowing to real sector that really need under the premise of total credit scale control. However, so far, it's still unclear whether it can achieve these goals or not.
3. In the new development stage, it is important to investigate the potential economic growth rate. If the economic growth rate target is higher than the potential economic growth rate, the macroeconomic costs may be greater than the benefits.

4.1 Reducing the Economic Growth Target

The main purpose of central government in the last 3 years was trying to maintain a stable growth rate above 7.5 % using micro-stimulus policies, but the marginal effect of micro-stimulus policies is diminishing. For each year, there existed a cyclical economic growth pattern: "decline—micro-stimulus—rebound—decline", and the length of the each cycle is becoming short year after year. And for each year, the starting time of micro-stimulus policies had to be shifted to an earlier time.

The experiences of China economy in the past 3 years show that, if the central government had not adopted the micro-stimulus policies, the economy would have grown slower than the actual growth rate, but frequently using micro-stimulus policies may create new problems. The short-term demand stimulus may only be used to smooth cyclical fluctuation, it is impossible to reach an economic growth rate higher than the nature growth rate in the long run. Frequently using micro-stimulus policy will inevitably lead to higher cost of macro-controls and operations, and ultimately loss is bigger than gain.

In the downstream stage of economic cycle, from the current economic development features, adapting to the economy of the new normal, keeping a normal attitude strategically, and setting a lower growth target will be beneficial to greatly reducing the cost of macro-control with less government intervention to economy. Therefore, it is an important issue need to investigate: whether it is more favorable to set a lower economic growth rate target. The theme of this CQMM policy simulation is: the effect of setting a lower economic growth rate target on major macroeconomic indicators.

For policy simulation, we imagine that the economic growth rate had been reduced to 7.2 % during 2012–2013.

4.2 Scenario Assumptions and Policy Effect Simulation

4.2.1 Scenario Assumptions

We assume the growth rate of Euro-zone and US economies keep the same over the 2 years, interest rate and exchange rate also remain unchanged, only money supply will vary with economic growth rate. We assume that the economic growth rate was 7.2 % rather than the actual value, 7.7 %. Accordingly, money supply could have been reduced. On one hand, less money supply would have led to the declines in investment, in the employment, in residential income growth, and in consumption growth; On the other hand, less money supply would have pulled down the price level, increased household real income, and promoted consumption. Moreover, with the lower economic growth target, incentive investment of local governments would have been relieved, the size of local government financing would have been reduced, which would have relieved the capital to the money market and played a positive role to private investment both in capital price and quantity supply. Therefore private investment cost would have declined, efficiency would have been improved and private investment would have been promoted, employment would have been increased and resident income would have been improved. The total effect (the positive effect together with the negative effect) is positive.

Shown in Fig. 4.1, the baseline and actual quarterly GDP growth rate almost keep the consistent trend, and the scenario assumption quarterly growth rate after the corresponding reduction in each quarter is lower than the actual (Fig. 4.1).[2]

[2]The CQMM is a quarterly model. Therefore, when substituted into the model, we need split the annual drop of economic growth into quarterly change. approach is: we first calculate the annual change of GDP after growth reduction, and then spilt the new annual economic data into new quarterly economic data based on the actual share of each quarter.

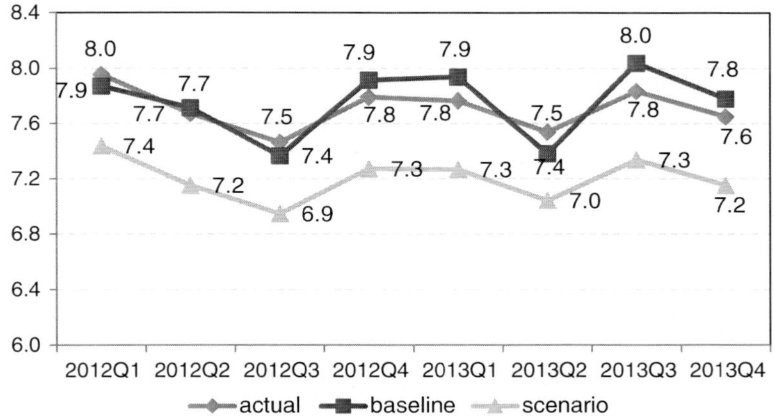

Fig. 4.1 The quarter economic growth rate after target adjustment (Note: actual denotes the real quarterly GDP growth rate; baseline denotes the baseline simulation quarterly GDP growth rate; scenario denotes the new quarterly GDP growth rate when the growth rate is downward adjusting to 7.2 % (year-on-year, after seasonal adjustment))

4.2.2 Policy Simulation Results

4.2.2.1 Change in M2 Growth Rate

In 2012 and 2013, image that the GDP growth had been reduced to 7.2 %, then M2 growth rate only would have been 11.7 % and 12.2 % respectively, decreases of 2.0 and 1.3 percentage points compared to the actual growth rate. Accordingly, M2 supply could have been reduced about 1.75 and 3.21 trillion CNY respectively. The cumulative change in each quarter of M2 growth rate is shown in Fig. 4.2.

4.2.2.2 Other Major Macroeconomic Indicators

First, compared to baseline, the growth rate of urban fixed asset investment would have declined about 2.5 and 2.3 percentage points respectively, in 2012 and 2013. The growth rate of manufacturing investment growth would have dropped 2.9 and 2.5 percentage points respectively; the growth rate of real estate investment would have dropped 2.5 and 2.3 percentage points respectively; and the growth rate of transportation infrastructure investment would have slightly declined 1.7 and 1.8 percentage points respectively. Affected by these, the proportion of manufacturing investment to the whole investment would have dropped by 0.1 and 0.17 percentage points respectively, and the proportion of real estate would have remained unchanged (Fig. 4.3).

Second, in terms of total retail sales of consumer goods, the growth rate would have dropped by about 0.3 and 0.7 percentage points in 2012 and 2013 respectively

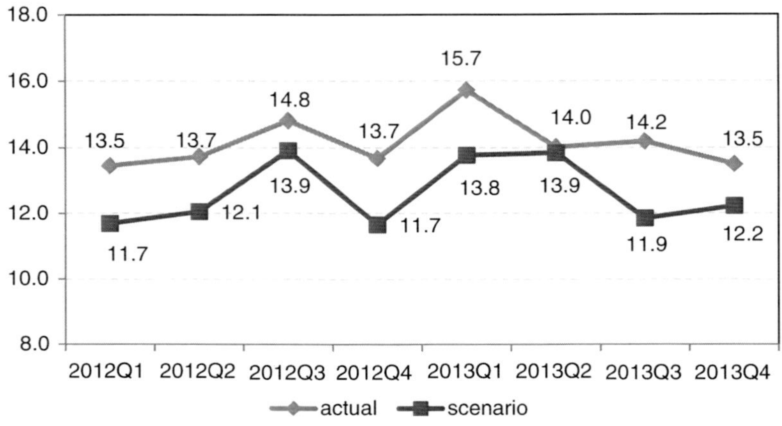

Fig. 4.2 Comparing with the actual and simulated M2 growth rate (Note: actual denotes the real M2 growth rate; scenario denotes the simulation M2 growth rate when the GDP growth rate is downward adjusting to 7.2 % (year-on-year, after seasonal adjustment))

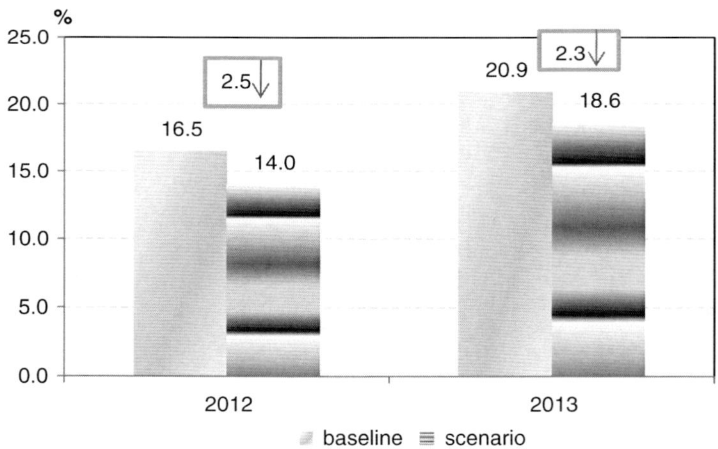

Fig. 4.3 The change of urban fixed asset investment (Note: baseline denotes the baseline simulation of urban fixed asset investment growth rate; scenario denotes the new urban fixed asset investment growth rate under scenario assumption (year-on-year, after seasonal adjustment))

compared to baseline, which is significantly smaller than the decline in investment growth rate. This is attributed to the fact that consumption is not directly affected by the impact of money supply, and may even be benefit from price decrease caused by less money supply. The consumer price index would have dropped by 0.09 and 0.16 percentage points respectively. In addition, the producer price index also would have dropped by about 0.47 and 0.82 percentage points (Fig. 4.4).

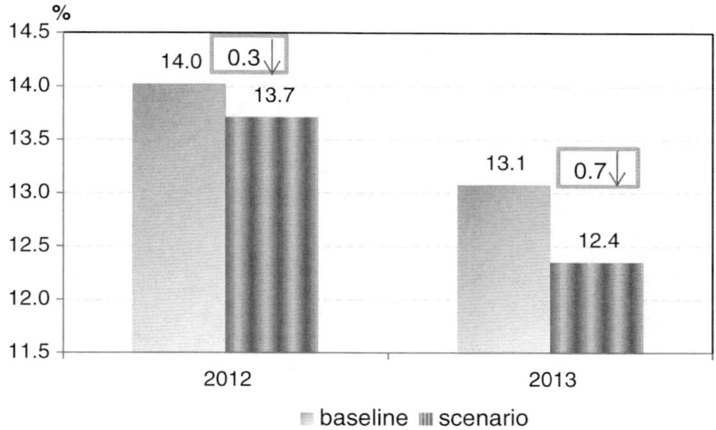

Fig. 4.4 The change of total retail sales of consumer goods (Note: baseline denotes the baseline simulation of total retail sales of consumer goods growth rate; scenario denotes the new total retail sales of consumer goods growth rate under scenario assumption (year-on-year, after seasonal adjustment))

Third, in terms of gross demand structure, due to the drop in investment growth rate, the proportion of gross capital formation to GDP would have dropped by 0.20 and 0.33 percentage points in 2012 and 2013 respectively; the proportion of household consumption increases by about 0.07 and 0.08 percentage points respectively; and owing to the decline of import, net export also would have increased by about 0.06 and 0.09 percentage points respectively. Overall, owing to investment decline, gross demand structure would have thus been slightly adjusted (Figs. 4.5, 4.6, and 4.7).

Fourth, in terms of employment, the downward adjustment of economic growth rate would not have brought a sharp decline to the growth rate of job creation in 2012 and 2013. The growth rate of new job positions would have dropped by only 0.13 and 0.19 percentage points respectively compared to baseline, which it's too tiny to affect the stability of the overall employment market (Fig. 4.8).

Finally, we conclude the results of policy simulation. If the economic growth rate had been reduced to 7.2 % in 2012 and 2013 respectively, then four results could be found: (1) the corresponding growth rate of M2 would have decreased to 11.7 and 12.2 %, which to some extent, would have helped to reduce the pressure of excess money supply; (2) it would have reduced the growth rate of urban fixed asset investment, a decrease of 2.5 and 2.3 percentage points respectively, which would have helped to relieve government investment pressure for stable growth, and then improved government financial situation and reduced the debt burden of government and the debt leverage ratio of enterprises; (3) the consumer price index would have declined by 0.09 and 0.16 percentage points respectively; (4) the most disturbing thing in the past, a significant reduction in employment, would have been not likely to occur. With the gradually expansion of service sector, which could have absorbed

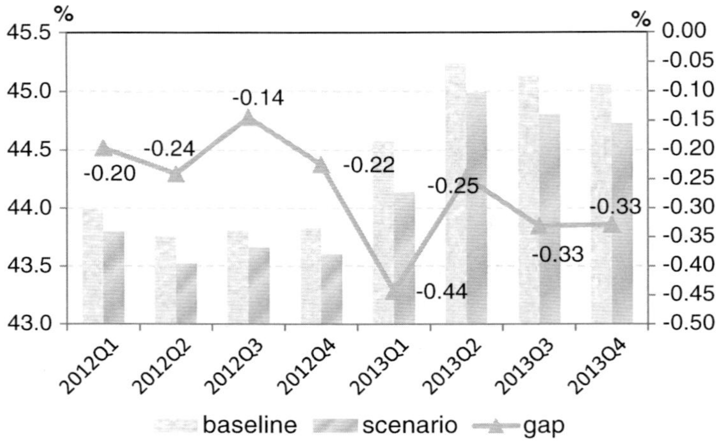

Fig. 4.5 The proportion change of gross capital formation to GDP (Note: baseline denotes baseline simulation; scenario denotes scenario assumption; gap denotes the difference between scenario and baseline (year-on-year, after seasonal adjustment))

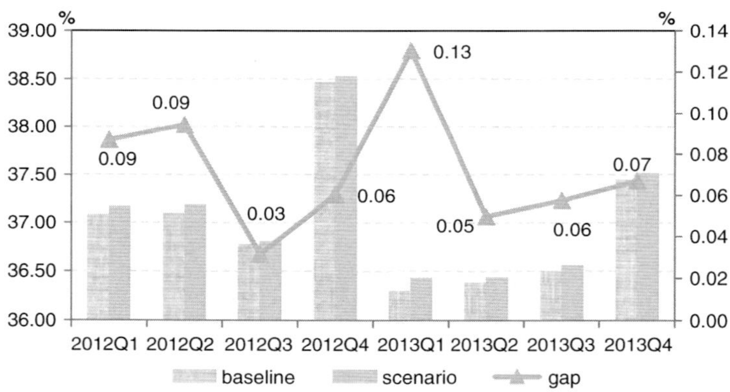

Fig. 4.6 The proportion change of household consumption to GDP (Note: baseline denotes baseline simulation; scenario denotes scenario assumption; gap denotes the difference between scenario and baseline (year-on-year, after seasonal adjustment))

more employment than manufacturing sector, the impact of a lower economic growth on employment is negligible; (5) in terms of gross demand structure, due to the drop in investment growth rate, the proportion of gross capital formation to GDP would have dropped by 0.20 and 0.33 percentage points respectively; the proportion of household consumption would have increased by about 0.07 and 0.08 percentage points respectively; and owing to the decline in import, net export also would have

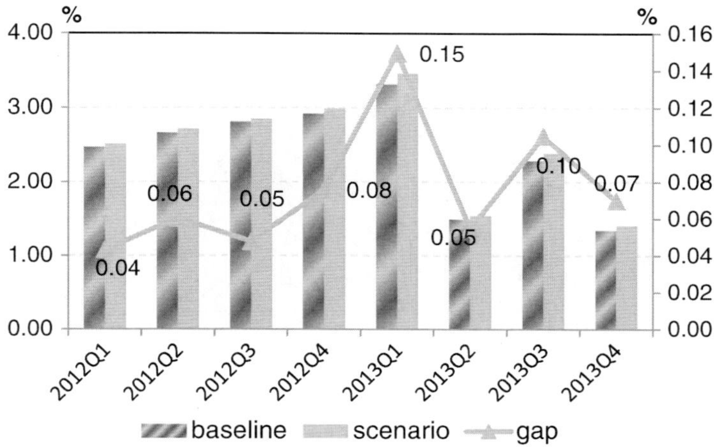

Fig. 4.7 The proportion change of net export to GDP (Note: baseline denotes baseline simulation; scenario denotes scenario assumption; gap denotes the difference between scenario and baseline (year-on-year, after seasonal adjustment))

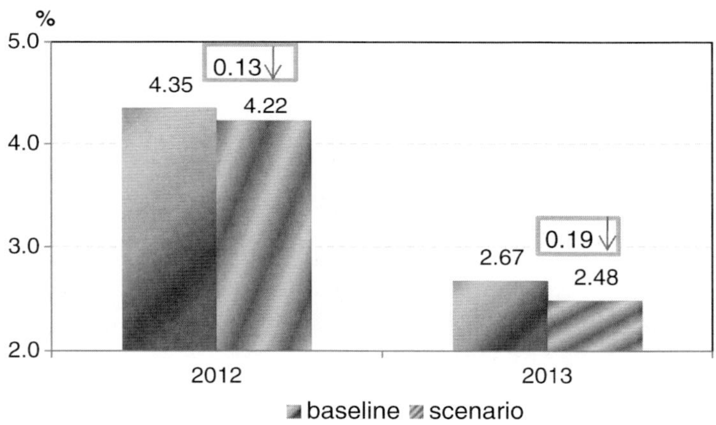

Fig. 4.8 The change of the growth rate of new added employed persons (Note: baseline denotes baseline simulation; scenario denotes scenario assumption (year-on-year, after seasonal adjustment))

increased by about 0.06 and 0.09 percentage points respectively. Overall, owing to investment decline, gross demand structure has thus would have been adjusted slightly.

Thus, we can conclude that the positive effect would have dominated the negative effects if economic growth rate have been reduced from 7.5 to 7.2 % under present circumstances.

Chapter 5
Conclusions and Suggestions

The slowdown of China's growth since 2008 is mainly because the old growth pattern was incompatible to the new environment, and also because the service sector replaced the manufacturing industries as the main driving force of economic growth. The economy is experiencing a transition period because of the global finance crisis. In the first quarter of 2014, the growth rate was 7.4 %, which was lower than the target. With a series of stimulus policies implemented by the central government, the economic growth picked up to 7.5 % in the second quarter, but downward pressure remains significant in the second half of 2014.

Turning to results predicted by the CQMM, in 2014, economic growth is expected to be 7.49 %. Quarterly, it is predicted to be 7.46 and 7.59 % in the third and fourth quarter, respectively. Therefore, the growth target of 7.5 % set by the central government is achievable. In 2015, economic growth will further decline to 7.36 %.

The constantly declining of economic growth has begun to suppress the growth of residential real income. The per capita disposable income of urban households only increased by 7 % in real terms in 2013, down 2.7 percentage points over the previous year, while the per capita net income of rural residents increased by 9.3 % in real terms, down 1.4 percentage points over the previous year.

In the first half of 2014, the per capita disposable income of urban households rose by 7.1 % in real terms, an increase of 0.6 percentage points compared to the same period of 2013, but a decrease of 2.6 percentage points compared to the same period of 2012. Meanwhile, the growth trend of the per capita cash income of rural residents is the same as that of urban households. However, the current macro-control policies, including micro-stimulus and targeted easing policies aiming at maintaining stable growth, are still focusing on investments rather than consumptions. As a result, the policy effect is insignificant either on changing the growth pattern or on increasing residential consumption.

In the next few years, should the central government insist on micro-stimulus policies to achieve the growth rate target of around 7.5 %, or abandon such stimulus policies gradually with a lower the growth rate target? This is a question to which special attention should be paid.

CMR of Xiamen University, *China's Macroeconomic Outlook*,
Current Chinese Economic Report Series, DOI 10.1007/978-3-662-45405-3_5

The marginal effect of micro-stimulus policies kept diminishing in the past 3 years, and the cost of macro-controls and operations kept rising, which indicates that the growth rate target of around 7.5 % is higher than the potential growth rate to a certain degree. In practice, maintaining a growth target higher than the potential growth rate with stimulus policies will drive up the costs of macroeconomic regulations and economic operations. Thus, if the central government insists on setting the growth rate target around 7.5 % for 2015 and 2016,[1] macro-control costs will be more expensive and policy effect will diminishing, and this is destructive to the efforts to deepen reforms, to adjust economic structure and to change the growth pattern. The reasons are listed below.

First, current growth rate of 7.5 % is based on excess money supply. In the first half of 2014, the scale of nongovernmental financing has reached 10.57 trillion RMB, the highest in the history, while M2 rose by 14.7 %. According to our forecast, the growth rate of M2 would reach 14.2 % in 2014, not only exceed the growth rate target of around 13 %, but also higher than 13.6 %, the actual level of previous year. Excess money supply in this year will bring about sluggish growth as well as inflation in the next year. What's more, if micro-stimulus policies are used in 2015, money supply excess will further aggravate, thus the pressure of inflation will further increase.

Second, if the central government sets a target of high growth rate, the efficiency of money will decrease. In the past 4 years (2010–2013), the marginal effect of money on output kept diminishing: For each additional 10,000 GDP, M2 must increase 16,700, 25,700, 26,500 and 32,500, respectively. In the first half of 2014, the growth rate reached 7.4 %, a decrease of only 0.2 percentage points over same period of the previous year, though the scale of financing increased by 420 billion RMB, 1.88 trillion RMB higher than the target set by the central government.

Third, the micro-stimulus and targeted easing policies are implemented mainly through expansion in infrastructure investment, resulting in efficiency decreasing of investment and debt growing of local governments. In the past 3 years, this policy focused on two fields: (a) infrastructure projects like railways, highways, public works, energy facilities, environmental engineering projects and water conservancy projects, which private capital was welcome to take part in; (b) construction of government-subsidized housing and reconstruction of rundown urban areas. All these investments made the government finance worsen.[2] The marginal effect of government debt on economic growth was diminishing. An additional one RMB of government debt created 0.53 RMB of GDP during 2005–2008, but only 0.29 during 2009–2013. With the current investment and financial system, if the central government sticks to a growth rate target of around 7.5 %, the cost of macro-controls and operations will be higher, local governments finance will be worsened,[3]

[1] So-called bottom line of growth.

[2] Micro-stimulus run by local governments may exceed six trillion, source from Economic Information, Xinhua Net, August 7, 2014: http://jjckb.xinhuanet.com/2014-08/07/content_515998.htm

[3] As our research team computes, the social debt ratio was 257 % at the end of 2012, essentially in agreement with the Asia Debt Investigation from the Standard Chartered Bank, July 21, 2014.

the resources and environment will bear more burden and the policy makers will face a more complex situation.

Fourth, setting a growth rate target as high as 7.5 % will not improve residential consumption. In the first half of 2014, economic growth declined by merely 0.2 percentage point, while the growth rate of retail sales of consumer goods decreased by 1.7 percentage points, compared to the same period of 2013. In particular, the sales of automobiles and furniture, the bellwether of economy, declined compared to the same period of previous year. Therefore, to maintain a higher growth rate would not be favorable to the consumption demand.

We suggest that the central government reduces the growth rate target from 7.5 % to around 7.2 % in 2015 and 2016, because such a modest growth target would be more beneficial. The reasons are as follows:

First, a lower growth rate will raise unemployment rate. One reason is that the new labor force is growth slowly because of the change the age structure of population, and the other reason is that the tertiary industry, which is employment friendly, is replacing the manufacturing industries as the driving force of the economic growth. The simulation indicates: if the growth rates in 2012 and 2013 both would have been reduced to 7.2 % from 7.65 to 7.67 %, the employment would have decreased slightly for about 167,000 persons for each year. In addition, the negative effect of lower growth rate would have been more insignificant if the expansion of the service sector had been considered.

The job-to-applicant ratio in China is 1.11, suggesting a robust demand in labor market, so setting a lower growth rate target of around 7.2 % in the next 2 years, will not affect the employment significantly.

Second, the simulation suggests that a lower growth rate target of around 7.2 % would be conductive to the major economic indicators to some degree.[4]

Third, a lower growth rate will also help to reduce the government debt. As the forecast, if economic growth rate is 7.1 % during the 13th five-year-plan, the government debt[5] will decrease about two trillion RMB in this next 5 years. Undoubtedly, it will have positive effects on alleviating the pressure of government debt.

Fourth, a lower growth rate target is easier to achieve, so the central government could be able to focus on more constructive tasks like deepening reforms, adjusting economic structure and changing the growth pattern rather without being disturbed by micro-stimulus policies. With the economic structural being adjusted, the potential growth rate will be higher, and the space for future growth will be larger.

In conclusion, the central government should give up the super high economic growth target, since the external economic growth is unlikely to pick up in the near future and the domestic economic system is yet to be further reformed and the growth pattern is yet to be changed. In our opinion, in the post crisis era, the central government should adapt to the economy of "new normal", take advantage of the situation, set a lower and reasonable growth rate target and lay a sound foundation for future growth.

[4] Turn to Chap. 4 for more details.

[5] In a broader sense, including debts with repayment liability, with guarantee liability and with rescue liability.

Chapter 6
A Survey of Chinese Economists on China's Macroeconomic Performance in 2014

(2014.8 · No. 3)

To keep abreast of the macroeconomic situation and policy trend, an annual questionnaire survey of China's macroeconomic situation and policy started in July 2014 for the third time, held by the Economic Information Daily from Xinhua News Agency and the Center for Macroeconomic Research, Xiamen University (one of the Key Research Institutes of Humanities and Social Sciences of the Ministry of Education of China). There are 16 questions directly about China's macroeconomic situation and policy trend in the questionnaire, and we invited some domestic economists in relevant area for this survey by email in early July, and finally got responses from 93 experts. The results of this survey are presented as follows:

6.1 The Main Downward Pressure on China's Macro-economy

Concerning the main downward pressure on China's macro economy, according to the survey, 68 % of experts answered with the slowdown of real estate industry investment growth and the year on year decreasing in the national commercial housing sales area, 62 % with the worsening problem of excess production capacity, 45 % with some systematic risks in financial institutions caused by the high risk of enterprises' debts, 44 % with the high risk of local governments' debt, 35 % with the continuous shortage of external demand. The results above showed that more than 60 % of experts claimed that the slowdown of real estate industry investment growth and the year on year decreasing in the national commercial housing sales area, the worsening problem of excess production capacity would be the major downward pressure, which were the crucial or important factors that would affect the healthy development of China's future economy. In addition, More than 40 % of experts maintained that the major downward pressure on China's economic development came from some systematic risks in financial institutions caused by the high risk of

CMR of Xiamen University, *China's Macroeconomic Outlook*,
Current Chinese Economic Report Series, DOI 10.1007/978-3-662-45405-3_6

enterprises' debts as well as the high risk of local governments' debt. In addition, nearly 40 % of experts argued that the continuous shortage of external demand would be the major downward pressure in China's macro-economy.

What's more, 19 % of the experts had different opinions on the major downward pressure including insufficient domestic demand (especially domestic consumption demand), the shortage of effective policy stimulation, all kinds of continuous structural contradictions, the declining growth rate of domestic consumption and fixed asset investment, serious nominal price distortions (totally beyond the sustainable allowance), the strengthening efforts against corruption and the increasing environmental pressure, the big gap in income distribution and the lack of industrial structure optimization, unclear direction of macroeconomic regulation, some personal expectations on economy downward pressure, spontaneous and disordering market competition, the lack of innovation, and the inaccurate way of government management, the type J downward pressure which happened in the process of industrial structure and economic structure transformation, the exit of QE, etc.

6.2 The Macroeconomic Situation of Euro Area and the United States in 2014

The economic growth rate of the United States was –2.9 % in the first quarter of 2014, dramatically beyond the market expectations, and has become the worst negative economic growth since the great depression happened in the first quarter of 2009. Comparing with its performance, what kind of trend will American economy have in 2014? In the 92 effective questionnaires to answer this question, the survey reflected that 27 % of the experts claimed that the economic growth rate of USA would increase "between 1.1 % and 2.0 %"; 24 % of them thought that it would be "between 0.1 % and 1.0 %"; 21 % said that it would be "between −1.9 % and −1.0 %"; 10 % forecasted that it would be "between –0.9 % and 0 %"; 10 % maintained that it would increase "2.1 % or more" and only 8 % chose "–2.0 % or less". Overall, overwhelming majority of the experts believed that the American economy would be in recovery, and the growth rate would increase in people's prediction, which situation would be relatively optimistic.

The growth rate of Euro-zone increased by 0.9 % year on year in the first quarter, which was higher than the previous quarter. Compared with the situation in the first quarter, what kind of trend will the economy of Euro zone have in 2014? The results showed that 61 % of the experts answered that the economic growth rate of Euro zone would increase "between 0.1 % and 1.0 %"; 38 % claimed that it would be "between 1.1 % and 2.0 %"; only 1 % of the experts thought that it would be "0.0 % or less" and no one said that it would increase "between 2.1 % and 3.0 %" or "3.1 % or more". In sum, overwhelming majority of the experts believed that the economy of Euro zone would be also in recovery and the situation would be relatively optimistic.

In regard to *USD/EUR exchange rate* in 2014, 56 % of the experts expected it would be "between 1.36 and 1.40"; 32 % considered that it would be "between 1.31 and 1.35"; 11 % chose "1.30 or less"; only 1 % claimed that it would be "between 1.41 and 1.50" and no one expected that it would be "1.50 or more". Hence, most of the experts forecasted a continuous trend of USD devaluation against EUR.

6.3 The Forecast of Some Major Indicators of China's Macro-economy in 2014

With respect to the growth rate of China's GDP in 2014, the survey showed that 73 % of the experts thought that it would be "between 7.1 % and 7.5 %"; 25 % expected that it would be "between 7.6 % and 8.0 %"; only 1 % maintained that it would be "7 % or less" and no one claimed that it would be "8.1 % or more". Moreover, one expert held different opinions, claiming that it would be "between 7.4 % and 7.6 %".In sum, 73 % of the experts considered that the growth rate in 2014 would be less than 7.5 % and the economic growth of China would slow down continually considering the growth rate of 7.4 % in the first half year of 2014.

In the first quarter of 2014, the job opening-to-application ratio of the public employment service agency in 102 cities in China is about 1.11, according to a survey conducted by the China's human resources market information monitoring center. Concerning the change of this ratio, 41 % of experts expected the rate in full-year of 2014 will be flat with the first quarter; 29 % claimed that compared with the first quarter, the employment situation might improve and this rate would rise; conversely, 20 % thought compared with the first quarter, employment situation might be worse and this rate would decrease. In addition, 10 % said that the variation of this rate seemed unclear. Overall, more than 40 % of experts believed that compared with the first quarter of 2014, the change of this rate would remain relatively stable in 2014. And 70 % held respectively optimistic attitude towards China's current employment situation.

Concerning the variation of China's CPI in 2014, the survey showed that 66 % of the experts expected it to be "between 2.1 % and 2.5 %"; 30 % thought that it might be "between 2.6 % and 3.0 %"; 4 % chose "between 3.1 % and 3.5 %"; meanwhile, no one claimed that it would be "2.0 % or less" or "3.6 % or more". Overall, nearly 2/3 of experts claimed that the price level would still stay steady and the inflationary pressure would continue to be lessened considering the fact that the CPI increased by 2.3 % in the past half year in 2014.

With regard to the growth rate of Producer Price Index (PPI) in 2014, the survey showed that 57 % of experts expected it to be "between −1.7 % and −1.0 %"; 17 % considered it would increase "between −0.9 % and 0 %"; 11 % chose "between 0.1 % and 0.9 %"; 11 % thought it might be "−1.8 % or less"; Only 4 % claimed that it would be "between 1.0 % and 1.9 %", and no one forecasted it would be "2.0 % or more". Considering the PPI dropped by 1.8 % year on year in the first half year in 2014, therefore, the results of the survey showed that most experts forecasted that the PPI would present a continuous uptrend in the next half year and full year of 2014.

In regard to the nominal growth of China's total retail sales of consumer goods in 2014, in the 92 effective questionnaires to answer this question, the survey showed that 68 % of the experts expected the total retail sales of consumer goods would increase year on year at the rate "between 12.1 % and 13.0 %"; 23 % considered that it would increase at the rate "less than 12.0 %"; 9 % chose "between 13.1 % and 14.0 %", and no one claimed that it would be "14.1 % or more". Considering the fact that the total retail sales of consumer goods grew by 12.1 % year on year in the first half year, the results reflected that most experts maintained that the growth of the total retail sales of consumer goods would be higher in the next half year and the full year of 2014 than the one in the past half year.

Regarding to the nominal growth of China's fixed investments (excluding farmers) in 2014, the survey showed that 55 % of the experts expected the total fixed investments would increase year on year at the rate "between 17.1 % and 18.0 %"; 23 % considered that it would increase at the rate "between 18.1 % and 19.0 %"; 16 % chose "17.0 % or less"; 6 % thought that the growth rate would be "19.1 % or more". Considering the fact that the total fixed investments grew by 17.3 % year on year in the first half year of 2014, it was clear that more than a half of experts claimed that the growth of China's fixed investments in the next half year would be higher than that one in the first half of 2014. However, when compared with the past year, the growth rate of China's fixed investments would slow down continually.

With respect to the nominal growth rate of the investments in real estate market in 2014, the survey showed that 80 % of the experts expected the total investments in real estate would increase year on year at the rate "14.0 % or less"; 15 % considered that it would increase at the rate "between 14.1 % and 15.0 %"; 5 % chose "between 15.1 % and 16.0 %", and no one claimed that it would be "16.1 % or more". In brief, most experts forecasted a continuous downtrend in China's real estate market in 2014 comparing with the situation in the past half year.

Concerning the situation of imports and exports in 2014, in the 92 effective questionnaires to answer this question, 79 % of the experts expected the total imports and exports would increase year on year at the rate "between 0.1 % and 5.0 %"; 20 % considered that they would increase at the rate "between 5.1 % and 8.0 %"; only 1 % chose "less than 0 %", and no one forecasted that they would be "between 8.1 % and 10.0 %" or "10.1 % or more" . Considering the fact that the total imports and exports grew by 1.2 % year on year in the past half year, the results reflected that 99 % of the experts claimed that the growth of the total imports and exports would decrease in 2014.

In regard to the USD to CNY (RMB) exchange rate in 2014, 41 % of the experts expected it would be "between 6.11 and 6.15"; 28 % considered that it would be "between 6.06 and 6.10"; 24 % chose "6.16 or more"; 6 % expected that it would be "between 6.01 and 6.05" and only 1 % claimed that it would be "6.00 or less". According to the financial statistics report issued by the people's bank of China in the first half of 2014, the USD to CNY exchange rate was 6.15 in late June. Hence, most of the experts forecasted a continuous trend of RMB appreciation against USD in the next half year.

Concerning the growth of China's broad monetary supply (M2) in 2014, 51 % of the experts had the expectation that M2 would grow at the rate "14.6 % or more"; 31 % considered "between 14.1 % and 14.5 %"; 11 % chose "between 13.6 % and 14.0 %"; 6 % maintained the views that the growth rate would be "between 13.1 % and 13.5 %", and only 1 % thought that it would be "less than 13.0 %". M2 grew at the rate of 14.7 % in June, 2014, so the survey reflected that more than 90 % of the experts claimed that the growth of M2 in 2014 would be higher than not only the predetermined target set at the beginning of the year, but also higher than the one in 2013.

6.4 Macroeconomic Policies Measures Might Be Implemented in the Second Half of 2014

With regard to the monetary policy measures which China might carry out in the second half of 2014, the results of the survey showed that 76 % of experts believed that China would maintain a small quasi-directional drop policy; 40 % claimed that China might cut interest rates once by the end of the year; 38 % argued that China might lower deposit reserve rate once by the end of year. Overall, nearly 80 % of experts forecasted that China would maintain a small quasi-directional drop policy in the next half year; 40 % thought China might cut interest rates once by the end of the year, and nearly 40 % believed that China might lower deposit reserve rate once by the end of year. In addition, 11 % of the experts had different opinions on monetary policy measures including: deposit rate marketization, maintaining a mild quantitative easing monetary policy, raising required reserve ratio and interest rates, increasing the amount of reloan and open market operations, carrying out comprehensive lowering deposit reserve rate policy and cutting interest rates at least once, flexible operation based on steady and robust principles, etc. Overall, most experts believed that monetary policy would maintain an appropriate loose tone in the next half year.

With regard to the fiscal measures China might take in the second half of 2014, 77 % of experts believed that China's government might moderately boost investment in new project and promote spending on infrastructure; 73 % claimed that China's government might implement preferential tax policies for small enterprises with low profits and carry out the fiscal and taxation policy which would promote the development of service consumption and enterprise innovation; 73 % thought China's government would continue to control "the three public expenses" and other general public spending; 70 % claimed that it would revitalize the stock of fiscal funds and increase the expenditure in people's livelihood security sector; 53 % answered that it might implement pilot programs to replace the business tax with VAT in more sectors and promote reform experiments in areas such as finance, telecommunications and postal service; 51 % claimed that it would build a finance mechanism for local government to borrow money, standardize the financing behavior, and establish a pre-warning system for debt risk; 38 % argued that it might increase the scale and proportion of general transfer payments and standardize the special transfer payments.

In addition, an expert gave his own opinion on the fiscal measures. He said that fiscal policies should serve the innovation, technological progress and human capital accumulation, etc. and all policies would be worthwhile to carry in order to achieve this goal. Overall, more than 70 % of experts believed that China's government might moderately boost investment in new project and promote expenditure on infrastructure, implement preferential tax policies for small enterprises with low profits and carry out the fiscal and taxation policy which would promote the development of service consumption and enterprise innovation, continue to control "the three public expenses" and other general public spending, revitalize the stock of fiscal funds and increase the expenditure in people's livelihood security sector. More than 50 % of experts claimed that it might implement pilot programs to replace the business tax with VAT in more sectors and promote reform experiments in areas such as finance, telecommunications and postal service, build a finance mechanism for local government to borrow money, standardize the financing behavior, and establish a pre-warning system for debt risk. Nearly 40 % of experts argued that it might increase the scale and proportion of general transfer payments and standardize the special transfer payments.

According to the Chinese Pinyin order of their names, the experts who joined this questionnaire survey were:

Chang Xin, Chen Changbing, Chen Gong, Chen Guifu, Chen Kunting, Chen Langnan, Chen Menggen, Chen Shoudong, Chen Yanbin, Chen Yongjun, Chen Zhiyong, Dai Yiyi, Deng Xiang, Fan Conglai, Fan Ziying, Gao Bo, Geng Qiang, Gong Gang, Gong Min, Guo Xibao, Guo Xiaohe, Guo Zhiyi, He Aiping, He Jingtong, Hu Jiayong, Jian Xinhua, Jiang Yongmu, Li Haizheng, Li Jianwei, Li Jing, Li Jun, Li Shi, Li Xiao, Li Xuesong, Li Yingdong, Liu Jianping, Liu Jinquan, Liu Renguo, Liu Yunzhong, Liu Zhibiao, Lu Shengrong, Lu Ming, Ma Ying, Peng Shuijun, Qiu Chongming, Shen Kunrong, Sun Wei, Tang Jijun, Tu Xinquan, Wang Changyun, Wang Tongsan, Wang Yida, Wang Cheng, Wang Haijie, Wang Jiping, Wang Jinzhao, Wang Meijin, Wang Ruifang, Wang Xin, Wang Yanwu, Wen Chuanhao, Wu Kaichao, Wu Xinru, Xiao Xingzhi, Xu Jianguo, Xu Yifan, Xu Wenbin, Xu Xianchun, Yang Zhiyong, Yin Xingmin, Yin Heng, Yu Li, Yuan Fuhua, Zeng Jinli, Zeng Kanghua, Zhang Liqun, Zhang Liancheng, Zhang Long, Zhang Ping, Zhang Yanqun, Zhang Yishan, Zhang Zhuoyuan, Zhao Jingxing, Zhao Zhenquan, Zhao Zhijun, Zheng Chaoyu, Zhong Chunping, Zhou Liqun, Zhou Zejiong, Zhu Baohua, Zhu Jianping, Zhu Qigui, Zhuang Zongming.

Experts and scholars to participate in the survey from:

Ministry of finance of China, National Bureau of statistics of China, Development Research Center of the State Council, National Academy of Economic Strategy, Chinese Academy of Social Sciences(CASS), Institute of Economics, CASS, Institute of World Economics and Politics, CASS, Institute of Quantitative and Technical Economics, CASS, Anhui University of Finance and Economics, Peking

University, Beijing Normal University, Chongqing Technology and Business University, Dongbei University of Finance and Economics, University of International Business and Economics, Fudan University, Hunan University, East China normal University, Huazhong University of Science and Technology, Jilin University, Jinan University, Lanzhou University, Nanjing University of Finance and Economics, Nanjing University, Nankai University, Shanghai Jiao Tong University, Capital University of Economics and Business, Sichuan University, Tianjin University of Finance Economics, Tianjin university of commerce, Wuhan University, Xiamen University, Xi'an Jiao Tong University, Northwestern University, Southwestern University of Finance and Economics, National University of Singapore, Yunnan University of Finance and Economics, Zhejiang University of Technology, Zhengzhou University, Renmin University of China, Zhongnan University of Economics and Law, Sun Yat-Sen University

Finally, we thank for the active participation and insights of these experts mentioned above sincerely.

Appendix

Forecasts of China's major macroeconomic indicators by the research team and 93 economists

China's major macroeconomic indicators for 2014	Forecasts of the research team (%)	Forecasts interval and the percentage of economists (%)	
		Interval	Percentage
Growth rate of the GDP	7.49	7.1–7.5	73
Growth rate of the CPI	2.51	2.1–2.5	66
Growth rate of the PPI	−1.53	−1.7–1.0	57
Nominal growth rate of total residents' consumption	12.61	12.1–13.0	68
Nominal growth rate of total fixed capital	17.12	17.1–18.0	55

MIX
Papier aus verantwortungsvollen Quellen
Paper from responsible sources
FSC® C105338

Printed by Books on Demand, Germany